FREE Test Taking Tips DVD Offer

To help us better serve you, we have developed a Test Taking Tips DVD that we would like to give you for FREE. **This DVD covers world-class test taking tips that you can use to be even more successful when you are taking your test.**

All that we ask is that you email us your feedback about your study guide. Please let us know what you thought about it – whether that is good, bad or indifferent.

To get your **FREE Test Taking Tips DVD**, email freedvd@studyguideteam.com with "FREE DVD" in the subject line and the following information in the body of the email:

> a. The title of your study guide.
>
> b. Your product rating on a scale of 1-5, with 5 being the highest rating.
>
> c. Your feedback about the study guide. What did you think of it?
>
> d. Your full name and shipping address to send your free DVD.

If you have any questions or concerns, please don't hesitate to contact us at freedvd@studyguideteam.com.

Thanks again!

Army Board Study Guide
Army Board Book and Practice Test Questions for the Army Promotion Board Hearing

Test Prep Books

Table of Contents

Quick Overview

As you draw closer to taking your exam, effective preparation becomes more and more important. Thankfully, you have this study guide to help you get ready. Use this guide to help keep your studying on track and refer to it often.

This study guide contains several key sections that will help you be successful on your exam. The guide contains tips for what you should do the night before and the day of the test. Also included are test-taking tips. Knowing the right information is not always enough. Many well-prepared test takers struggle with exams. These tips will help equip you to accurately read, assess, and answer test questions.

A large part of the guide is devoted to showing you what content to expect on the exam and to helping you better understand that content. In this guide are practice test questions so that you can see how well you have grasped the content. Then, answer explanations are provided so that you can understand why you missed certain questions.

Don't try to cram the night before you take your exam. This is not a wise strategy for a few reasons. First, your retention of the information will be low. Your time would be better used by reviewing information you already know rather than trying to learn a lot of new information. Second, you will likely become stressed as you try to gain a large amount of knowledge in a short amount of time. Third, you will be depriving yourself of sleep. So be sure to go to bed at a reasonable time the night before. Being well-rested helps you focus and remain calm.

Be sure to eat a substantial breakfast the morning of the exam. If you are taking the exam in the afternoon, be sure to have a good lunch as well. Being hungry is distracting and can make it difficult to focus. You have hopefully spent lots of time preparing for the exam. Don't let an empty stomach get in the way of success!

When travelling to the testing center, leave earlier than needed. That way, you have a buffer in case you experience any delays. This will help you remain calm and will keep you from missing your appointment time at the testing center.

Be sure to pace yourself during the exam. Don't try to rush through the exam. There is no need to risk performing poorly on the exam just so you can leave the testing center early. Allow yourself to use all of the allotted time if needed.

Remain positive while taking the exam even if you feel like you are performing poorly. Thinking about the content you should have mastered will not help you perform better on the exam.

Once the exam is complete, take some time to relax. Even if you feel that you need to take the exam again, you will be well served by some down time before you begin studying again. It's often easier to convince yourself to study if you know that it will come with a reward!

Test-Taking Strategies

1. Be Prepared

It is best to make sure that you have everything ready to go the night before your promotion board hearing. This will help make sure that you don't forget anything on the day of. It will also be helpful to give yourself extra time to get ready on the day of. Consider giving yourself an extra 30 minutes to an hour longer than usual.

2. Stay Relaxed but Alert

You have been preparing for this moment now for a while. You have a good idea of what to expect and have prepared answers for as many questions as you can. There is nothing left to worry about so try to just be relaxed and confident as you enter the room. You should still remain alert and make all of the appropriate movements, but just try not to appear stiff and nervous.

3. Listen to the Whole Question

Too often, candidates will hear a question, recognize a few familiar words, and immediately jump to a wrong answer. The promotion board will notice this and it will have a negative impact on your review. For instance, they might subtly turn the question into a negative, or they might redirect the focus of the question right at the end. The only way to avoid falling into these traps is to listen to the entirety of the question carefully before forming your answer.

4. Your First Instinct

As mentioned, you have been preparing for this for a while now. You have formed answers for most of the questions that will be ask and you have memorized your unit history, creed, and current events. When the question is asked, just go with your first instinct and speak in a strong, clear voice.

5. Answer Truthfully

Don't be afraid to not know the answer to a question that is ask. There are a lot of things to memorize for this hearing. It is better to give an answer like "1SG, I do not recall the answer to that question at this time", rather than trying to make a wild guess or lie your way through the hearing. You can also give a partial answer like "1SG, I do not recall the exact answer to your question but I know that it is covered in AR 750-1".

FREE DVD OFFER

Don't forget that doing well on your exam includes both understanding the test content and understanding how to use what you know to do well on the test. We offer a completely FREE Test Taking Tips DVD that covers world class test taking tips that you can use to be even more successful when you are taking your test.

All that we ask is that you email us your feedback about your study guide. To get your **FREE Test Taking Tips DVD**, email freedvd@studyguideteam.com with "FREE DVD" in the subject line and the following information in the body of the email:

- The title of your study guide.
- Your product rating on a scale of 1-5, with 5 being the highest rating.
- Your feedback about the study guide. What did you think of it?
- Your full name and shipping address to send your free DVD.

Introduction

Function of the Test

The Army Promotion Board is for soldiers in the U.S. army who are ranked E-4 or E-5 and eligible for a promotion. Those who are eligible will have the appropriate grade, operational experience, and training benchmarks. Soldiers in the primary zone will automatically be recommended, while those in the secondary zone will need unit commanders to recommend them.

Test Administration and Format

Soldiers facing the Army Promotion Board will conduct the following actions in order:

- Line-Up
- Enter
- Facing Movements
- Biography
- Board Questions
- Unit History/Creeds/Current Events
- Dismissal

About three questions per subject will be asked during the Board Questions portion of the exam over information in the Memorandum of Instruction (MOI).

Scoring

Soldiers who pass the Army Promotion Board will need to earn 798 out of 800 maximum points in the categories of Military Training, Military Awards and Decorations, Military Education, and Civilian Education. In order to be promoted, the Corporal (CPL) or Specialist (SPC) must meet MOS cutoff score, complete Structured Self Development (SSD) prior to board appearance, pass a promotion board review, graduate the Basic Leader

Course (BLC), and have 36 months TIS and 8 months TIG for primary zone, and 18 months TIS and 6 months TIG for secondary zone.

In order to be promoted, the Sergeant (SGT) must meet MOS cutoff score, complete SSD prior to board appearance, pass a promotion board review, graduate the Advanced Leader Course (ACL), have 72 months TIS and 10 months TIG for primary zone, and 48 months TIS and 7 months TIG for secondary zone.

Recent/Future Developments

In the May 2018 promotion moth, a policy went into effect which allows soldiers to automatically be eligible for the promotion recommendation list, whether or not they've caught their command's attention.

Overall Promotion Process

Line-Up

The Army Promotion Board has a variety of participants. The board might include competition board and promotion board candidates, or there might only be promotion board candidates in attendance. Sponsors also attend the board alongside their candidates. The president of the board presides over the proceedings, and there are always several additional board members present. In addition, a recorder assists the board.

When they initially arrive, all the candidates and sponsors wait in a designated area until the president of the Army Promotion Board calls everyone into the room. The president then gives orders on how the candidates and sponsors should line up in the room. Typically, candidates for promotion stand in straight rows in front of the board, and the sponsors are positioned behind their candidate.

After the attendees are properly arranged in the line-up, the president will deliver a brief introduction, discuss the requirements for promotion, and conduct a visual examination. For example, the president might check the candidates' uniform measurements or ask the candidates to present identification. Candidates should make sure to bring both their ID cards and ID tags.

Once satisfied, the president concludes the line-up by dismissing all the candidates and sponsors. The candidates and sponsors then return to the waiting area until the next phase begins.

Entering

The candidates are individually called back into the board from the waiting area. If both competition board and promotion board candidates are in attendance, then the competition board candidates are called first. The promotion board candidates will follow, and the order is based on rank, with junior candidates appearing before senior candidates.

When the recorder calls out a candidate's name, that candidate's sponsor enters the board room first. The board briefly questions the sponsor about the candidate's achievements, qualifications, and other circumstances of the promotion. Sponsors typically remain in front of the board for no more than a few minutes.

After the board has finished questioning the sponsor, the recorder calls the candidate, instructs the candidate to wait 10 seconds before knocking, shuts the door, and returns to their seat.

The candidate knocks three times, waits for the president's command, opens the door, closes the door without turning their back to the board, and heads directly toward the president. The candidate must stop at arm's length from the president, salute, and say "SPC ___ reporting to the president of the board." The candidate must wait until the president's hand fully descends before dropping their own.

The entering phase then concludes with several general questions. For example, the president might ask the candidate about their day or recent assignments.

Facing Movements

Candidates perform facing movements as requested by the president or other board members. The purpose of these movements is twofold. First, the board evaluates how the candidate appears while performing the movements. Second, the different movements allow the board to inspect the candidate's uniform. The president will instruct the candidate to execute movements in front of every board member so they can individually judge the candidate's uniform.

Candidates should not speak during this phase unless a board member directly asks a question. For example, if the board members are discussing a candidate's uniform discrepancy amongst themselves, that candidate should not interrupt unless asked about the discrepancy. After the end of the facing movements phase, the president orders the candidate to have a seat in their designated chair.

Biography

The biography phase begins once the candidate takes their seat, remaining at attention. The purpose is for the board to get an idea about the candidate's background, ambitions, and thought process. The biography is unique in that it represents the only opportunity for the candidates to showcase their personal story, which is why many candidates believe this phase is so critical.

Prior to the board, candidates should prepare a brief speech that relates their upbringing, path to the Army, short-term goals, and long-term goals. It is a good idea for candidates to discuss how this promotion will serve those goals. For example, the short-term goal could be to work in a capacity that requires the promotion, and the long-term goal could be a higher rank.

Candidates must be honest with the board, and candidates should remain as calm as possible because the board is judging how they maintain their composure under pressure. Whenever speaking, candidates should always maintain eye contact with each board member.

Board Questions

The board questions can cover any material in the Memorandum of Instruction (MOI), and all the board members participate in this phase. The range of questions is broad, and questions differ from one candidate to another.

Question types are entirely dependent on what the board members decide to ask in that moment. However, every subject listed on the MOI will be addressed, and, generally speaking, there are approximately three questions per subject. The number of questions per subject can change based on performance. For example, if the candidate does not answer the first two questions correctly, then the board might ask three additional questions.

The breadth of the questions can be nerve-wracking, but it is important to remember that the board doesn't want to fail candidates. It is unreasonable to expect a candidate to have an encyclopedic knowledge of the MOI and the ability to recall every detail in a tense situation. So even if the questions are obscure, candidates should remain calm. Remember the board is promoting soldiers, not doctoral students, so keeping cool under pressure is very important. When candidates are struggling, board members might offer a hint, and they will want to help candidates who maintain an exceptional presentation and demeanor even if they are providing incorrect answers.

If the candidate does not know the answer, they should say, "First Sergeant, I cannot recall the answer to this question right now." Candidates should also offer whatever information they have. For example, in the circumstances described above, a better response would be, "First Sergeant, I cannot recall the answer to this question right now, but I do remember the answer can be found under Army Regulation X." As with keeping calm, candidates who demonstrate some knowledge are more likely to receive hints from board members. However, candidates must tailor the additional information specifically to the question. For example, an inappropriate response would be, ""First Sergeant, I cannot recall who the United States fought in

World War I, but I do remember the United States fought Spain in the Spanish-American War."

Unit History, Creeds, and Current Events

This phase is the board's next-to-last one, and it is the last phase based on the board's questions and the candidate's answers. Candidates should be prepared to answer questions about their unit's history and creeds. In addition, the president may ask questions about recent global events.

The history questions are broad. At a minimum, candidates should be prepared to explain the history of their unit's badges. Questions could relate to the badges' design, location, or introduction. Another major topic is the unit's origin story and history in major conflicts or historical periods.

Candidates need to recite several creeds, including the soldier's creed, the noncommissioned officer (NCO) creed, and any creeds specific to the unit. Of the three, recitation of the NCO creed is held to the highest standards, though all the creeds should be recited perfectly. Failing to adequately recite the NCO creed when the candidate is an NCO or seeking a promotion to NCO is grounds for disqualification.

The president's other questions test the candidate's general understanding of recent global events. Candidates are not expected to understand every intricacy of geopolitics, but they should be informed about major armed conflicts and related political disputes, particularly those involving the United States. Reading the world affairs section of a major newspaper for several months is typically sufficient, unless the candidate is entirely unfamiliar with global events.

Dismissal

The dismissal phase begins after the president concludes their questions and asks the candidate if they have anything they'd like to ask or tell the board. Candidates can use this time to correct wrong answers from the previous phase. For example, if you forgot the date the Civil War ended, you could say, "I would like to use this opportunity to correct my answer to First Sergeant's question. First Sergeant, the Civil War ended on April 9, 1865."

After the candidate finishes their final statement, the president will tell the candidate they are dismissed. When the candidate hears they are dismissed, they should stand up, walk over to the president, position themselves an arm's length away, and render a hand salute. The president will then return the salute, and the candidate must hold their salute until the president completely drops their hand.

Following the salute, the candidate leaves the room. The candidate's sponsor remains in the room for a brief period, and the board members provide him with feedback. After all the candidates have completed the board, the president calls everyone back into the room to announce promotions and competition winners, if applicable.

Content with Questions and Answers

Profession

Leadership

The Army defines **leadership** as providing purpose, direction, and motivation in order to accomplish missions and improve the whole organization. Purpose gives a soldier reason to act. Clear direction requires communicating information about a mission, including the priority of tasks, specific responsibilities, and standards. Motivation is the strength of will that's required to accomplish the mission. Army leadership is covered in Field Manual 6-22 (FM 6-22).

In matters of leadership, the Army follows the expression "be, know, and do." Being a leader means holding the Army values of loyalty, duty, respect, selfless service, honor, integrity, and personal courage. Knowing how to be a leader has to do with knowledge and competency. A leader must apply their values and knowledge to effectively lead. Army leaders can amplify their effectiveness through military bearing, physical fitness, confidence, and resilience.

Leaders can develop their soldiers through effective communication, especially through engaging in counseling, coaching, and mentoring. Effective communication is vital for overcoming physical and psychological barriers to critical learning. The three domains for critical learning are: institutional training, operational experiences, and self-development. All training should involve stress to simulate the conditions necessary for victory and survival on the battlefield.

Leadership has three different levels: direct, organizational, and strategic. **Direct leadership** occurs face to face, for example, during one-on-one counseling sessions. **Organizational leadership** involves a significant number of people, numbering in the hundreds or thousands, and it is conducted by delegating authority to subordinates. **Strategic leadership** is the broadest leadership level, occurring at the level of the major commander through Department of Defense, and decisions at that level can impact the entire Army.

Army leaders are problem solvers. The seven steps for solving a problem are: identifying the issue, gathering information, developing criteria, brainstorming potential solutions, analyzing those solutions, comparing those solutions, and implementing the decided-upon solution. When analyzing solutions, leaders should always be aware of intended and unintended consequences.

Counseling

Leaders must conduct counseling to review their subordinates' performance and potential avenues for improvement. The objective of **counseling** is to help soldiers meet their potential, which strengthens the unit. Providing counseling services for subordinates is mandatory for all Army leaders. FM 6-22 Appendix B provides an overview of the counseling process, and the appropriate form is DA Form 4856-E.

There are four phases in the counseling process. First, the leader identifies a subordinate in need of counseling. Second, the leader prepares for counseling by notifying the subordinate, selecting an appropriate time and place, and outlining a strategy. Third, the leader and subordinate participate in the counseling session. Fourth, the leader conducts a follow-up with the subordinate.

Effective counseling requires purpose, flexibility, respect, and communication. The purpose of the counseling program or counseling session must always be clearly defined. The style of counseling must be flexible and tailored to each subordinate.

The subject of counseling must always be respected as a unique and complex individual with their own personal set of values, beliefs, and attitudes. Counselors should particularly focus on active listening and tactful questioning.

There are three approaches to counseling: directive, nondirective, and combined. **Directive counseling** is the quickest type of counseling, but it does not involve the subordinate in the process. Examples of directive counseling include corrective training and commands. **Nondirective counseling** increases the subordinates' capacity for self-development, but it is time-consuming and requires a skilled counselor. **Combined counseling** is a middle ground approach in which the counselor includes the subordinate in the process but also issues directives. Leaders engaging in nondirective or combined counseling should suggest alternatives, make recommendations, present persuasive arguments, and advise the subordinate.

There are three types of developmental counseling: event counseling, performance counseling, and professional growth counseling. Examples of event counseling include performance reviews, reception and integration counseling, referral counseling, crisis counseling, promotion counseling, and separation counseling.

Chain of Command

The **chain of command** refers to how command is exercised, flowing from superiors to subordinates. Command includes authority and responsibility. Authority is transferred from superiors to subordinates, and subordinates have a responsibility and a duty to follow orders passed down through the chain of command.

Commanders exercise command by delegating their authority to subordinate commanders, who are responsible for ensuring that orders are followed.

The sergeants' primary responsibilities are related to training and leading soldiers, commonly referred to as Sergeant's Business. As a result, sergeants must have the skill, ability, and leadership to prepare and lead soldiers into combat.

Command sergeant majors (CSMs) are battalion commanders or senior enlisted advisors to the commanders. CSMs are not formally in the chain of command, but they are responsible for supervising NCOs, who act as a sergeant's support channel in the context of chain of command.

The NCOs' primary responsibility is to support sergeants, which they can do by legally punishing soldiers who violate a sergeant's command. The NCO support channel was formally recognized within the chain of command on December 20, 1976.

NCO Duties, Responsibilities, and Authority

Responsibilities bring accountability for actions, including a failure to act. All soldiers have individual responsibilities and command responsibilities. Individual responsibility is accountability for personal conduct, while command responsibility is accountability for a unit's performance. An NCO's two most important responsibilities are mission accomplishment and looking after the welfare of their soldiers. Specifically, the bulk of an NCO's duties and responsibilities involve training and maintaining discipline. However, responsibilities differ based on context, such as the mission and whoever is delegating the authority. FM 7-22.7 handles the duties, responsibilities, and authorities of an NCO.

Soldiers also have specified, directed, and implied duties. **Specified duties** are based on jobs and positions, and they are derived from Army regulations, soldier's manuals, Department of Defense publications, and so on. **Directed duties** come directly from superiors, and they are handed down orally or in writing. **Implied duties** support specified duties, but they aren't necessarily related to the soldier's job or position. They may not be written explicitly. Instead, implied duties improve the quality of life, improve the work environment, or increase motivation.

Authority is a leader's legitimate power to direct authority. **Command authority** is exercised based on rank or assignment, and the highest level of command authority lies with the president of the United States. **Military authority** is a broader concept, allowing soldiers to unilaterally act without the presence of a leader or other authority. For example, if a soldier notices someone violating an order or disobeying the law, then military authority allows the soldier to intervene.

Power means having the ability to exercise positive control over other people's actions, and it can be the product of physical, mental, or moral abilities. The Army has five categories of power: legal, reward, coercive, referent, and expert. **Legal power** is based on law and regulation. **Reward power** entails providing desirable rewards when a soldier succeeds. **Coercive power** forces people to behave in a different manner than they otherwise would. **Referent power** is the ability of a leader's personality to inspire respect and admiration amongst their soldiers, which is why referent power is sometimes called charismatic power. **Expert power** is the product of knowledge, skills, and capabilities.

Supervision is checking to make sure orders are being implemented correctly. A strong leader considers his soldiers' competence, motivation, and commitment to the task. Supervision should not be confused with harassing soldiers, which can harm performance. The four basic steps of supervision are: assign a task, set standards, check progress, and follow up to determine whether those standards have been met.

NCO History

The use of noncommissioned officers (NCOs) in the Army dates back to the founding of the Continental Army in 1775. Prussian officer Baron Friedrich von Steuben's "Blue Book" (1778) first standardized NCOs' duties and responsibilities. Von Steuben classified NCOs as corporals, sergeants, first sergeants, quartermaster sergeants, and sergeants major. During the Revolutionary War, Sergeant Elijah Churchill, Sergeant William Brown, and Sergeant Daniel Bissell were all awarded the Badge of Military Merit, which was a precursor to the Medal of Honor.

The chevron is the symbol of NCO rank, and the War Department first used it in 1821. The chevron was modified to its current form in 1902. The training of NCOs was improved in 1829 after the publication of "The Abstract of Infantry Tactics." An influential but unofficial publication, "The Noncommissioned Officers Manual," was published in 1909. The Army issued standards for NCO academies in 1950 (AR 350-90). The E8 and E9 grades were created in 1958 to clarify NCOs' responsibilities and improve the structure of enlisted soldiers.

The sergeant major of the Army (SMA) is the second most senior enlisted Army NCO. The position of sergeant major of the Army was created in 1966, and Sergeant Major William O. Wooldridge was the first to serve in this capacity. As of February 2019, there have been fifteen SMAs, and the three most recent SMAs have been Sergeant Major of the Army Kenneth O. Preston (2004-2011), Sergeant Major of the Army Raymond F. Chandler (2011-2015), and Sergeant Major of the Army Daniel A. Dailey (2015-present).

The Senior Enlisted Advisor to the Chairman of the Joint Chiefs of Staff (SEAC) is the most senior NCO in the entire Armed Forces, holding an E-9. The Chairman of the Joint Chiefs of Staff appoints the SEAC, and the SEAC represents enlisted personnel within the Department of Defense. CSM William Gainey was appointed as the first ever SEAC on October 1, 2005, and CSM John W. Troxell currently serves in this role as of February 2019.

Army Programs

The Army Substance Abuse Program (ASAP) aims to strengthen the Army's fighting force by rehabilitating soldiers. Participation is mandatory when soldiers are referred to ASAP, and failure to participate in the program will result in an administrative separation and a possible violation of Article 86 of the Uniform Code of Military Justice (UCMJ). AR 600-85 governs ASAP.

The Army Community Service (ACS) is intended to strengthen soldiers, civilian staff, and their families by improving the services they receive. Volunteers primarily run ACS, and the program's motto is "self-help, service, and stability." AR 608-1 governs ACS.

The Army Continuing Education Center (ACES) provides opportunities for soldiers to pursue educational advancement for the purpose of supporting the enlistment, retention, and transition of soldiers. The tuition assistance grant covers 100% of tuition, and ACES offers Pell Grants, Perkins Loans, and Guaranteed Student Loans.

The Army Emergency Relief (AER) supports soldiers and their families by providing emergency financial assistance.

The Army Sexual Assault Prevention and Response Program seeks to eliminate sexual assault by raising awareness, increasing prevention, conducting training, promoting victim advocacy, and holding perpetrators accountable. The Army's sexual assault policy applies on and off post, regardless of whether the soldier is on duty.

Equal Opportunity (EO) aims to eliminate discrimination and support teamwork. Every commander is required to publish an EO policy statement. EO is covered in AR 600-20 Chapter 6.

The Army Family Action Plan (AFAP) was created in 1983 to facilitate the communication of family issues with Army leadership. AR 608-47 addresses AFAP.

The Army Red Cross (ARC) helps soldiers communicate with their families and prepare for emergencies. In addition, ARC conducts blood drives and offers CPR instruction, swimming lessons, transportation services, financial assistance, counseling referrals, and health and safety services. ARC is covered in AR 930-5.

The Army Reenlistment and Retention Program helps maintain the fighting force. Soldiers may not reenlist if they have been barred by an administrative action or enrolled in ASAP. Soldiers must reenlist for 3 years to qualify for a Selective Reenlistment Bonus (SRB).

The Army Safety Program ensures safety is a responsibility held by every soldier. Special emphasis is placed on reducing carelessness, which causes the majority of accidents. AR 385-10 governs safety, and accidents are reported under AR 385-40.

The Army Sponsorship Program is available for soldiers leaving a unit. The program has six elements: DA Form 5434.M, Welcome Letter, ACS Relocation Readiness Services, Reception, Orientation, and In-Processing.

The Army Quality of Life Program (QOLP) aims to improve soldiers' living conditions and duty environment. The program's guiding principle is that the soldier is the Army's most important resource. The ACS and AER are examples of the QOLP.

The Better Opportunities for Single Soldiers (BOSS) improves the life of soldiers living without families; BOSS's purpose is to increase and sustain morale. The BOSS council has a president, vice-president, secretary, and treasurer.

The Civilian Health and Medical Program (CHAMPUS) assists family members of active duty, deceased, and retired military personnel in finding in-patient and out-patient care.

The Defense Enrollment Eligibility Reporting System (DEERS) issues dependent ID cards for eligible family members, such as a spouse and children.

The Noncommissioned Officer Development Program (NCODP) helps NCOs become better leaders by strengthening their skills, knowledge, and abilities.

Army and Joint Force

The United States is committed to defending the homeland, maintaining an effective presence overseas as a deterrent, conducting simultaneous campaigns all over the world, and thwarting the threat posed by weapons of mass destruction (WMD) and terrorism. The Joint Force is responsible for executing this multi-pronged strategy, and the leader of the Joint Force is called the Joint Force Commander.

Elements of the Joint Force include the Army, Navy, Air Force, Marine Corps, Coast Guard, Special Operations Command, Reserve components, and civilians, including senior leadership and support staff. The Joint Force is based on the principle of interdependence, meaning it purposefully relies on sub-elements' services and joint capabilities. As such, every element must be well organized, highly trained, and capable of being integrated with other elements.

Title 10 of the United States Code outlines the responsibilities and obligations for the Joint Force's elements. The Army is responsible for providing the Joint Force with sufficient land power to win wars and create enduring peace. The Department of the Army is one of three military departments (along with the Navy and the Air Force) within the Department of Defense. The Secretary of the Army leads the Department of the Army, and it is a civilian position appointed by the president and confirmed by the Senate. The highest-ranking military officer is the Chief of Staff of the Army, who is a member of the Joint Chiefs of Staff, who advise the president on military strategy and the Joint Force's capabilities.

Leaves and Passes

There are many different types of leave. **Accrued leave** is gained through service time, while **Advanced leave** is granted before the soldier has enough accrued leave. **Annual leave** is ordinary leave, meaning it comes out of a soldier's accrued days, while **Convalescent leave** doesn't detract from the soldier's leave account because it is prescribed. The maximum number of days for **Reenlistment leave** is ninety days, as long as Advanced leave exceeds thirty days. Soldiers are allowed to take a maximum of forty-two days of leave after the birth of a child, but if they voluntarily choose to take less than forty-two days, then they must receive approval from a physician.

Emergency leave is limited to emergencies involving the soldier's immediate family, and it counts against the soldier's leave account. Commander will authorize payment for air transportation when a soldier takes emergency leave, but the emergency leave transportation will take the soldier to the Aerial Port of Debarkation (AOD) that is closest to the emergency.

An administrative absence is authorized only when it benefits the Department of the Army. Permissive temporary duty authorization (PTDY) is granted by the installation or equivalent commander, and it is an excused absence for an educational, career-related, or participation in a semi-official or official Army program. PTDY cannot be combined with annual leave, so there must be a duty day in between the two leaves. Terminal leave refers to the termination of a soldier's service in the Army.

Passes are shorter than leave and unrelated to a soldier's leave account. Passes are a privilege, and they can be denied if the commander doesn't believe the soldier deserves a pass. A three-day pass may be obtained for typical workweek duty. For example, a soldier could receive a 3-day pass from Monday through Wednesday. However, a four-day pass cannot include more than 2 days where the soldier is on duty. Passes may not be combined with leave.

AR 600-8-10 deals with the leaves and passes, and DA Form 31, commonly referred to as a Leave Form, is the way soldiers request authority for leave.

Promotions and Reductions

The Army promotion system aims to recognize the most qualified soldiers, strengthen the unit, retain talented soldiers, and provide an objective and equitable process. There are three levels of promotion: unit, semi-centralized, and DA centralized. AR 600-8-19 governs enlisted promotions and reductions.

Factors that should be considered when recommending a soldier for promotion include overall performance, attitude, demonstrated leadership, and develop potential. Soldiers should be promoted only when they already have the skills and abilities required to perform all their new position's duties and responsibilities.

Soldiers' promotion points are recalculated on an annual basis. If a soldier is not recommended for promotion despite being eligible without a waiver, then the leader must conduct a counseling session on where the solder can improve to reach the next grade. Only two waivers can be requested when recommending a soldier for promotion.

A soldier may request an administrative reevaluation after accruing twenty or more points since their last promotion. When a soldier requests a reevaluation, they are first eligible for that promotion on the first day of the third month after the PSC receives the request. Total reevaluations also consider administrative points but they differ in that the entire process is reviewed from recommendation through the promotion board. Soldiers may request a total reevaluation 6 months after appearing before the promotion board or last reevaluation.

The promotion board must include at least three voting members and a recorder who may not vote. Any officer or NCO may sit on the board, but every member must be more senior than the candidate for promotion. The president of the board is the board's most senior member.

Soldiers may be administratively reduced for: erroneous enlistment grade, misconduct, inefficiency, an Other Than Honorable discharge, and failure to complete the required training. Inefficiency refers to the soldier being unable to satisfactorily perform their current grade's duties and responsibilities. Soldiers can be reduced for misconduct by Article 15, court-martial, and civil court conviction.

Communications

Communications Security (COMSEC) is an integral part of Operations Security (OPSEC). There are five methods of communication: radio, sound messages, visual messages, messenger, and wire. Sending by messenger is the most secure method of communication.

Radio is the least secure method of communication. Radios can be affected by weather, terrain, antenna strength, power, and location, particularly in altering a radio's range. The majority of infantry radios are FM modulated. Signal Operation Instructions (SOI) involve organizing stations into nets, assigning call signals and frequencies, alternating frequencies, designating Net Control Stations (NCS), and issuing security procedures for radio operators. To increase security, soldiers should listen and determine if the net is clear before submitting a radio message. FM 24-18 provides information on Tactical Single-Channel Radio Communications Techniques.

An Army/Navy Portable Radio Communicator (AN/PRC) is a small unit transceiver radio used by squads. An AN/PRC-77 weighs approximately 25 pounds, and it has an estimated range of 5 to 8 kilometers where it can broadcast its 920 channels.

Wire Drum (WD-1) is communications field wire. WD-1 wire should be used by giving approximately 20% slack. Under hard-packed dirt roads, the wire should be buried somewhere between 6 to 12 inches, but if the soil is loose or sandy, the wire should be buried at least 3 feet. W-1 wire must be repaired with a square knot. A single "donut roll" contains 1/2 mile of WD-1, and there is 1/4 mile on a DR8 reel.

TA-1 field phones have an approximate range of 3.7 miles when utilizing field wire. TA-312 field phones have a maximum effective distance of 14 miles in wet climates and 22 miles in dry climates. TA-312 field phones have a common battery (CB), local battery (LB), and common battery signaling (CBS).

Sample Questions and Answers

1. How does the Army define leadership?

The Army defines leadership as providing purpose, direction, and motivation in order to accomplish missions and improve the whole organization.

2. Who can receive assistance through CHAMPUS?

The Civilian Health and Medical Program (CHAMPUS) assists family members of active duty, deceased, and retired military personnel to find in-patient and out-patient care.

3. What responsibilities are common to all soldiers?

Every soldier has individual responsibilities and command responsibilities. Individual responsibilities refer to personal conduct, and command responsibilities involve the unit's performance.

4. What is accrued leave?

Accrued leave is gained through service time.

5. What is required for counseling to be effective?

Effective counseling requires purpose, flexibility, respect, and communication.

6. What is AR 600-8-19?

AR 600-8-19 governs enlisted promotions and reductions.

7. What elements are included in the Joint Force?

The Joint Force includes the Army, Navy, Air Force, Marine Corps, Coast Guard, Special Operations Command, Reserve components, and civilians, including senior leadership and support staff.

8. Who can obtain an identification card through DEERS?

Eligible dependent family members, such as a spouse and children, can receive identification cards from Defense Enrollment Eligibility Reporting System (DEERS).

9. How are directed duties handed down to subordinates?

Subordinates receive directed duties directly from superiors orally or in writing.

10. What is the Army's seven-step approach to problem solving?

First, the soldier must identify the issue. Second, the soldier must gather information. Third, the soldier must develop criteria for potential solutions. Fourth, the soldier must brainstorm potential solutions. Fifth, the soldier must analyze the potential solutions. Sixth, the soldier must compare the solutions with each other. Seventh, the soldier must implement the decided-upon solution.

11. What role did Sergeant Major William O. Wooldridge play in NCO history?

Sergeant Major William O. Wooldridge was the first sergeant major of the Army after the position was created in 1966.

12. What level of leadership has the broadest impact?

Strategic leadership has the broadest impact because those decisions can impact the entire Army. In contrast, direct leadership occurs face to face, and organizational leadership only impacts hundreds or thousands of soldiers.

13. Who holds the highest level of command authority over the United States military?

Under Article II of the Constitution, the president of the United States serves as the Commander in Chief of the Armed Forces, so the president holds the highest level of command authority over the United States military.

14. What is AR 600-85?

AR 600-85 includes the policies and procedures involved in the Army Substance Abuse Program (ASAP).

15. What must be overcome for leaders to effectively communicate with soldiers?

Effective communication requires overcoming physical and psychological barriers.

16. What should be considered when recommending a soldier for promotion?

Soldiers should be recommended for promotion based on overall performance, attitude, demonstrated leadership, potential, and ability to perform all the duties and responsibilities required by the new position.

17. Where does the Army drop off soldiers taking emergency leave?

Emergency leave transportation will take the soldier to the Aerial Port of Debarkation (AOD) that's closest to the emergency, not directly to the emergency location.

18. Which Army program conducts blood drives and offers CPR instruction, transportation services, and financial assistance?

The Army Red Cross (ARC) conducts blood drives and offers CPR instruction, transportation services, and financial assistance.

19. What is the Army's responsibility to the Joint Force?

The Army is responsible for providing the Joint Force with sufficient land power to win wars and create enduring peace.

20. What are the four phases of counseling, from beginning to end?

First, the leader identifies the subordinate who needs counseling. Second, the leader prepares for counseling, notifies the subordinate, selects an appropriate place and time, and outlines a counseling strategy. Third, the leader conducts the counseling session with the subordinate. Fourth, the leader follows up with the subordinate.

21. Where do command sergeant majors stand in the chain of command?

Command sergeant majors are not formally in the chain of command; instead, they are responsible for supervising NCOs' support of sergeants within the chain of command.

22. What was the Badge of Military Merit?

The Badge of Military Merit was awarded during the Revolutionary War, and it was a precursor to the Medal of Honor. Sergeant Elijah Churchill, Sergeant William Brown, and Sergeant Daniel Bissell received the Badge of Military Merit during the Revolutionary War.

23. What are the responsibilities of an NCO in the chain of command?

The NCO's responsibilities include supporting sergeants by maintaining discipline, conducting the training needed to accomplish missions, and looking after the welfare of their soldiers.

24. What is BOSS?

Better Opportunities for Single Soldiers (BOSS) improves the life of soldier living without families; BOSS's purpose is increasing and sustaining morale.

25. Who is the highest-ranking military officer in the Army?

The Chief of Staff of the Army is the highest-ranking military officer in the Army, and they are a member of the Joint Chief of Staff, which advises the president on military strategy and the Joint Force's capabilities.

26. What is the quickest type of counseling?

Directive counseling is the quickest type of counseling because it involves commanding and corrective training. In contrast, nondirective counseling and combined counseling feature a longer dialogue between subordinates and leaders.

27. Who is the current sergeant major of the Army?

As of February 2019, the current Sergeant Major of the Army is SMA Daniel A. Dailey.

28. What is a sergeant's primary responsibility?

Sergeants' primary responsibilities are related training and leading soldiers, which is also called Sergeant's Business.

29. How many donut rolls are needed to lay 1 mile of WD-1?

Two donut rolls because a single "donut roll" contains 1/2 mile of WD-1.

30. What is the minimum rank for a member of the promotion board?

There is no minimum rank required to sit on the promotion board, but every member must be more senior than the candidate for promotion.

31. Why does a soldier need to check the net before sending a radio message?

Checking the net is a counterintelligence measure intended to thwart the enemy's spies and increase the security of radio operations, which is the least secure method of communication.

32. What duties are based on jobs and positions?

Specified duties are based on jobs and positions, and they are derived from statutes and official publications, like Army regulations, soldier's manuals, Department of Defense publications, etc.

33. When must a leader conduct a counseling session during the promotion process?

A leader must conduct a counseling session when a subordinate soldier is not recommended for promotion despite being eligible without a waiver, and the counseling session focuses on where the soldier can improve to reach the next grade.

34. What is PTDY?

Permissive temporary duty authorization (PTDY) is an excused absence for an educational, career-related, or participation in a semi-official or official Army program, and it is granted by the installation or equivalent commander.

35. What does AN/PRC stand for?

It stands for Army/Navy Portable Radio Communicator (AN/PRC), and it is a small unit transceiver radio used by squads.

36. What happened on December 20, 1976?

On December 20, 1976, the NCO support channel was formally recognized within the chain of command.

37. How do Army leaders provide direction to soldiers?

Leaders provide direction to soldiers by communicating information about a mission, such as the priority of tasks, specific responsibilities, and standards.

38. What is the Joint Force's guiding principle?

The Joint Force is based on the principle of interdependence, meaning it purposefully relies on sub-elements' services and joint capabilities.

39. Separation counseling is an example of what?

Separation counseling is an example of event counseling. Other examples of event counseling include performance reviews, reception and integration counseling, referral counseling, crisis counseling, and promotion counseling.

40. What form of communication is most affected by conditions on the ground?

The form of communication that is most affected by conditions on the ground is radio, because it is the least secure and reliable method of communication since it can be affected by weather, terrain, antenna strength, power, and location.

41. What is the difference between an administrative reevaluation and a total reevaluation?

An administrative reevaluation is based strictly on a soldier having accrued twenty or more administrative points since their last promotion, while a total reevaluation reviews the entire process from recommendation through the promotion board.

42. What is the "Blue Book"?

Prussian officer Baron Friedrich von Steuben published the "Blue Book" in 1778, and it was the first publication to classify Army NCOs and standardize their duties and responsibilities.

Von Steuben classified NCOs as corporals, sergeants, first sergeants, quartermaster sergeants, and sergeants major.

43. What is the difference between taking leave and receiving a pass?

Passes are a privilege, while leave is a right. In addition, passes are shorter in duration than leave and don't detract from a soldier's leave account.

44. What does FM 7-22.7 cover?

FM 7-22.7 handles the duties, responsibilities, and authorities of an NCO.

45. What is DA Form 31?

DA Form 31 is known as the Leave Form, and it is the way soldiers request authority for leave.

46. What are the six elements of the Army Sponsorship Program?

The six elements of the Army Sponsorship Program are: DA Form 5434.M, Welcome Letter, ACS Relocation Readiness Services, Reception, Orientation, and In-Processing.

47. Which types of counseling involves making recommendations, presenting persuasive arguments, and advising subordinates?

Nondirective and combined counseling involve making recommendations, presenting persuasive arguments, and advising subordinates.

48. What two publications most influenced the development of NCOs between the years 1800 and 1950?

"The Abstract of Infantry Tactics" (1829) and "The Noncommissioned Officers Manual" (1909) influenced the development of NCOs before the Army issued standards for NCO academies in 1950.

49. How does the chain of command function?

The chain of command refers to the way command flows from superiors to subordinates after the delegation of authority.

50. What is the Army's expression for leadership?

The Army follows the expression "be, know, and do" for leadership. Being a leader means holding Army values. Knowing how to be a leader requires knowledge and competency. Doing leadership involves applying the values and knowledge to effectively lead.

History

Military Justice

The Articles of War was the first law to govern military justice in the United States, and it was active until Congress passed the Uniform Code of Military Justice (UCMJ) in 1950 to create a military justice system. The UCMJ contains 146 articles and twelve sub-articles. The UCMJ allows for three different types of courts-martial: Summary Courts-Martial, Special-Courts Martial, and General Courts-Martial. When facing accusations related to a matter of military justice, Article 31 provides soldiers with the right to remain silent, the right to an attorney, and the right to demand trial.

The UCMJ covers nonjudicial punishment in Article 15. Different types of **Article 15s** include Summarized, Company Grade, and Field Grade. Any commanding officer can charge a soldier with an Article 15, but a Field Grade Article 15 must come from at least an O4 officer. Company commanders can issue the following maximum punishments: fourteen days of extra or restricted duty, 7 days of correctional duty or forfeited pay, and one Grade Reduction for junior soldiers below E4. However, an NCO can only be assigned extra supervisory duty. A soldier does not have to accept an Article 15; instead, the soldier may demand a trial by court-martial unless they are currently aboard a ship.

The United States Court of Appeals for the Armed Forces is the highest American military court, and it regularly meets in Washington DC. The court initially had three civilian judges, but Congress expanded the court to five judges in 1990. All the civilian judges are appointed by the president and confirmed by the Senate.

Code of Conduct

President Dwight D. Eisenhower's administration first issued the **Code of Conduct (COC)** on August 17, 1955, and it was later amended in May 1988. The Eisenhower administration was seeking to strengthen the resolve of American POWs. The COC is expressed in AR 350-30 and reinforced by the Manual for Courts-Martial (UCMJ). The COC is supported by Survival, Evasion, Resistance, and Escape (SERE) training, which prepares soldiers for hostile environments.

The COC has six articles. Article 1 states that a soldier is prepared to sacrifice their life to protect their country, and Article 2 says the soldier vows to never surrender unless resistance is futile. Article 3 requires POWs to resist and attempt escape by any means necessary, and it prohibits the acceptance of parole or special favors from the enemy. Article 4 appoints the senior POW as the leader and requires fellow POWs to follow the lead POW's lawful commands. Article 5 requires American POWs to provide captors with their name, rank, service number, and date of birth, but it also prohibits

POWs from issuing disloyal statements. Article 6 details how soldiers should be dedicated to the United States.

Geneva Convention

The **Treaty of Amity and Commerce** (1778) between the United States and Kingdom of Prussia was the first international agreement to require the humane treatment of POWs. It was written by Benjamin Franklin, Thomas Adams, and Thomas Jefferson. The humane treatment of POWs was later reinforced by the Geneva Convention. At the time of its original drafting during the aftermath of World War II, sixty-one nations attended the August 12, 1949 conference in Switzerland. In total, the Geneva Convention incorporates four treaties and three additional protocols. The four treaties related to POWs were written simultaneously, and they are known as the Geneva Conventions for the Protection of War Victims. The United States ratified the Geneva Convention on February 2, 1955. DA PAM 27-1 ensures the Army's adherence with the Geneva Convention.

Only a "competent tribunal" of the capturing nation can determine a POWs status. Medical personnel and chaplains accompanying the American Armed Forces are not considered POWs. Amongst other requirements contained in the Geneva Convention's 143 articles for the treatment of POWs, the Geneva Convention prohibits violent treatment, cruel treatment, torture, and humiliating and degrading treatment. In addition, the Geneva Convention grants POWs a series of rights, including the right to freely worship and the right to retain identification and personal documents. For minor offenses, the maximum nonjudicial punishment for a POW is: 30 days confinement, extra duties, and loss of privileges. If no senior captured officers are present, POWs are allowed to elect a representative by secret ballot every 6 months. POWs may write a capture card to notify next of kin about their status and health. The **Geneva Convention** states that the main duty of a POW is to escape and help fellow POWs escape. Junior enlisted

POWs may be forced to perform physical and mental labor, but NCOs may only be required to perform supervisory duty; however, NCOs can be asked to do other work. American soldiers who deliberately violate the Geneva Convention are subject to court-martial under the UCMJ. POWs must salute the enemy camp commander even if they are not an officer.

United States Constitution

Signed on September 17, 1787, the **United States Constitution** replaced the ineffective Articles of Confederation and became the highest law in the United States. The US Constitution contains a preamble and seven articles, and it establishes the executive, judiciary, and legislative branches of government, which are co-equal.

The **preamble** introduces the document, establishes its purpose, and begins with the famous words "We the people of the United States." **Article I** establishes the Legislative Branch. **Article II** establishes the Executive Branch. The president of the United States unilaterally leads the Executive Branch and serves as the Commander in Chief of the American Armed Forces. **Article III** establishes the Judiciary Branch. **Article IV** covers the obligations and rights of the states under this federal system of government. **Article V** states the process for passing amendments to the Constitution. **Article VI** contains the Supremacy Clause, which elevates federal laws above state and local laws as long as the federal law doesn't violate the Constitution. **Article VII** governs how the US Constitution must be ratified.

The first ten amendments to the US Constitution are collectively referred to as the **Bill of Rights**, and they were simultaneously ratified on December 15, 1791.

The **First Amendment** protects a number of individual rights, including the freedom of religion, free speech, free press, right to peaceful protest, and right to petition the government. The

Second Amendment establishes the right to bear arms. The **Third Amendment** prohibits the government from forcing citizens to "quarter" (house) soldiers during wartime. The **Fourth Amendment** protects against unreasonable searches and seizures, requiring a warrant based on probable cause. The **Fifth Amendment** provides several protections for criminal trials, such as the protections against self-incrimination, double jeopardy, and seizure of private property. The **Sixth Amendment** further expands the rights of criminal defendants, but they don't apply to court-martial proceedings. The **Seventh Amendment** protects the right to trial by jury in civil cases. The **Eighth Amendment** protects against excessive fines as well as cruel and unusual punishment. The **Ninth Amendment** establishes the existence of rights that aren't specifically named in the US Constitution. The **Tenth Amendment** reserves all unnamed powers to the states or the people unless it violates the Constitution.

In total, there have been twenty-seven amendments to the US Constitution. Only one amendment has ever been repealed. In that instance, the **Eighteenth Amendment** (Prohibition) was repealed by the **Twenty-First Amendment**. The most recent amendment, the **Twenty-Seventh Amendment**, was ratified in 1992; it prohibits changes to Congressional salaries from taking effect until the next term begins.

Army History

Prior to the establishment of the US Army, the Massachusetts Bay Colony formed the Army National Guard in December 1636. The modern US Army was established on June 14, 1775, during the **Revolutionary War**, which began on April 19, 1775. George Washington served as the Army's first commander in chief. The Declaration of Independence was signed on July 4, 1776. Thus, in a sense, the Army is older than the United States.

During the winter of 1778 at Valley Forge, the Prussian officer Baron Friedrich von Steuben led the Army's first official training session on formations, movements, bayonets, senior leadership, and the importance of NCOs. Von Steuben also published the "Blue Book," which served as the US Army's field manual until General Winfield Scott published "The Army Regulations of 1821."

Significant wars undertaken by the US Army include the **Mexican-American War** (1846–1848). The United States fought Mexico over territorial disputes in the present-day American Southwest. The **Civil War** began on April 12, 1861 when Confederate ships bombed Fort Sumter in Charleston Harbor, South Carolina. Abraham Lincoln issued the Emancipation Proclamation on September 22, 1865, as a wartime measure to free the slaves held in Confederate territory. The **Battle of Gettysburg** began on July 1, 1863, and it marked a turning point in the war. Confederate General Robert E. Lee surrendered to Union General Ulysses S. Grant on April 9, 1865 at Appomattox Court House, Virginia, effectively ending the war. The Civil War resulted in 600,000 American deaths between the two sides, making it the bloodiest war in American history.

On April 25, 1898, Congress declared war on Spain; the **Spanish-American War** lasted until August 13, 1898. As a result, Spain ceded Cuba, Puerto Rico, Guam, and the Philippines to the United States. On June 28, 1914, the assassination of Archduke Franz Ferdinand of Austria-Hungary triggered events that led to World War I. After Germany refused to stop its policy of unrestricted submarine warfare and offered to help Mexico invade the United States, President Woodrow Wilson asked Congress to declare war on April 2, 1917. World War I ended on "Armistice Day," November 11, 1918, which is currently celebrated as Veteran's Day in the United States.

On December 7, 1941, Japan launched a surprise attack on Pearl Harbor. Congress declared war on Japan and Germany on December 8 and December 11, 1941, respectively. The United States launched an amphibious invasion of Normandy on June 6, 1944 ("D-Day"). The 1st, 4th, and 29th Infantry Divisions assaulted Utah and Omaha beaches at first light. On May 7, 1945, Germany officially surrendered, and President Harry S. Truman authorized the deployment of atomic weapons on Hiroshima and Nagasaki on August 6 and August 9, 1945, respectively. Japan announced its surrender on August 15, 1945, ending **World War II**. The Women's Army Corps was created during World War II (1943).

Following the end of World War II, Congress passed the National Security Act of 1947 to reorganize the American Armed Forces, creating the Department of Defense, Army, Navy, and Air Force. On June 25, 1950, North Korea invaded South Korea, and the United Nations dispatched security forces to assist South Korea. Hostilities ended on July 27, 1953, but no peace treaty was ever signed between the combatants. The Army flag was approved on June 12, 1956 and dedicated on June 14, 1956. President John F. Kennedy increased American involvement in Vietnam in 1960, and after the 1964 Gulf of Tonkin incident, President Lyndon B. Johnson further escalated the conflict. The conflict was the longest in American history, and the United States withdrew from Vietnam on January 27, 1973.

After Iraq invaded Kuwait in 1990, US Army General Norman Schwarzkopf led an international coalition into Iraq in February 1991, effectively ending the conflict. On September 11, 2001, Al Qaeda terrorists attacked the United States, and the George W. Bush administration responded by launching a war against Afghanistan on October 7, 2001. On March 20, 2003, the United States invaded Iraq to remove Saddam Hussein from power, and he was executed on April 9, 2003. President Barack Obama withdrew the bulk of American troops from Iraq by December 2011.

Sample Questions and Answers

1. What was the first law to govern military justice in the United States?

The Continental Congress passed the Articles of War in 1775, making them the first law to govern military justice in the United States.

2. What type of treatment of POWs does the Geneva Convention prohibit?

The Geneva Convention prohibits torture, violent treatment, cruel treatment, and the humiliating and degrading treatment of POWS.

3. What does Article II of the U.S. Constitution establish?

Article II establishes the Executive Branch.

4. What is SERE?

Survival, Evasion, Resistance, and Escape (SERE) prepares soldiers for hostile environments, including how to evade capture and how to resist and escape captivity, all while supporting the Code of Conduct.

5. What is the Supremacy Clause?

Contained in Article VI of the U.S. Constitution, the Supremacy Clause elevates federal laws above state and local laws as long as the federal laws do not violate the Constitution.

6. What is Article 15?

Article 15 governs nonjudicial punishment under the UCMJ.

7. Which constitutional amendment was later repealed?

The only constitutional amendment to have ever been repealed is the Eighteenth Amendment (Prohibition).

8. What did the United States gain at the end of the Spanish-American War?

Spain ceded control over Cuba, Puerto Rico, Guam, and the Philippines to the United States at the end of the Spanish-American War.

9. What does the Code of Conduct prohibit POWs from accepting?

Article 3 of the Code of Conduct prohibits POWs from accepting parole or special favors.

10. Whose presidential administration withdrew the bulk of American troops from Iraq?

The Obama administration withdrew the bulk of American troops from Iraq by December, 2011.

11. What is DA PAM 27-1?

DA PAM 27-1 ensures the Army's adherence to the Geneva Convention.

12. Where did Confederate General Robert E. Lee finally surrender to the Commanding General of the United States Ulysses S. Grant?

Confederate General Robert E. Lee surrendered to Union General Ulysses S. Grant at Appomattox Court House, Virginia on April 9, 1865.

13. When was the United States Court of Appeals for the Armed Forces expanded to five judges?

Congress expanded the United States Court of Appeals for the Armed Forces from three to five judges in 1990.

14. What were the events that led to the United States entering World War I?

Germany refused to stop its policy of unrestricted submarine warfare and offered to help Mexico invade the United States. These events ultimately led to President Woodrow Wilson asking Congress to declare war on Germany.

15. How many extra days of duty can a company commander impose on a subordinate?

Company commanders can impose a maximum of fourteen days of extra duty on a subordinate.

16. How many days of confinement can be imposed on a POW for minor offenses?

The maximum nonjudicial punishment for a POW is thirty days of confinement for minor offenses.

17. Which event led to President Lyndon B. Johnson escalating the Vietnam War?

The Gulf of Tonkin incident led to President Lyndon B. Johnson further escalating the Vietnam War in 1965.

18. What is AR 350-30?

AR 350-30 establishes the Code of Conduct.

19. When did the Mexican-American War take place?

The United States fought the Mexican-American War from 1846 until 1848 over territorial disputes in the present-day American Southwest.

20. Which rights are protected in the Fifth Amendment?

The Fifth Amendment protects the rights of criminal defendants; it includes protections against self-incrimination, double jeopardy, and unlawful seizure of private property.

21. What was the Treaty of Amity and Commerce?

The Treaty of Amity and Commerce (1778) was a trade agreement between the United States and Kingdom of Prussia, and it was the first international agreement to require the humane treatment of POWs. Benjamin Franklin, Thomas Adams, and Thomas Jefferson helped negotiate and write the Treaty of Amity and Commerce.

22. Which rights are protected by the First Amendment?

The First Amendment protects a number of individual rights, including the freedom of religion, freedom of speech, freedom of the press, the right to peaceful protest, and the right to petition the government.

23. What is Article 5 of the Code of Conduct?

Article 5 of the Code of Conduct prohibits POWs from issuing disloyal statements. In addition, Article 5 requires POWs to provide captors with their name, rank, service number, and date of birth.

24. How many treaties and protocols are incorporated in the Geneva Convention?

The Geneva Convention incorporates four treaties and three additional protocols.

25. Which UCMJ Article provides accused soldiers with the right to remain silent?

Article 31 of the UCMJ provides soldiers with the right to remain silent, the right to an attorney, and the right to demand a trial.

Service

Physical Training

The purpose of physical training is to prepare soldiers for war. Physical training is broken down into three phases: preparatory, conditioning, and maintenance. The preparatory phase is 2 weeks, while the conditioning phase ends when soldiers meet all their fitness-related goals and they are prepared for missions. Regardless of the phase, exercise routines include warm-up, conditioning, and cool-down. The Army breaks down physical fitness into five categories: cardio-respiratory endurance, muscular strength, muscular endurance, flexibility, and body composition.

Physical fitness takes place in either extended rectangular or circular formations. Fitness tasks fall into four different categories: collective tasks, individual tasks, leader tasks, and resources for training. Master Fitness Trainers (MFTs) design and implement the Army's fitness training programs. MFTs are certified after completing a fitness training program, and they hold expertise in creating both individual and unit fitness programs. Most training programs correspond with the FITT acronym (frequency, intensity, time, and type). In addition, programs are designed in accordance with the seven principles of exercise: regularity, progression, overload, balance, specificity, variety, and recovery.

The minimum score for each event at the **Army Physical Fitness Test (APFT)** is sixty points, and there must be at least one scorer for every fifteen soldiers present. Soldiers who are 55 or older may take the alternate APFT, which includes push-ups, sit-ups, and an aerobic exercise. An APFT failure will not prevent a soldier from receiving an award.

Physical training is referenced in a variety of places. The Army Physical Fitness Program is detailed in AR 350-1, Chapter 1, Section 24. Physical fitness training is addressed in FM 21-20. The Physical Profile Form can be found in DA Form 3349. The Physical Readiness Test Scorecard is DA Form 705.

Weight Control

The overriding purpose of the **Army Weight Control Program** is to guarantee that all soldiers are combat ready and have a proper military appearance. The Army believes excess body fat shows a lack of discipline, undermines military appearance, and indicates poor health and/or fitness.

AR 600-9 defines the body fat standards used to determine if soldiers are overweight, and those standards apply to every soldier, including commissioned officers. However, the Department of Defense has set a more rigorous goal of 18% body fat for males and 26% body fat for females, which all soldiers should aspire to achieve. Unit commanders and supervisors screen their soldiers to determine if their body fat needs to be tested. Weight-screening tables based on height and age are used to identify soldiers who might be in violation of AR 600-9. Otherwise soldiers should be weighed after taking the APFT or every 6 months at a minimum. The tape test is used to measure a soldier's body fat, and the test must be conducted with a non-stretchable tape measure, such as fiberglass. Male soldiers are measured at the abdomen and neck, while females are measured at the neck, waist, and hip. Two people are needed to conduct the test, and every measurement must be done three times.

If a soldier has more fat than is allowed under AR 600-9, their unit commander or supervisor will enroll them in a weight control program, which begins as soon as the soldier is told about their enrollment. Soldiers in the program have a monthly weight loss goal of 3 to 8 pounds, depending on circumstances, and they must be weighed on a monthly basis. Along with entering the weight control program, overweight soldiers must receive extra exercise and dietary guidance, behavioral modification counseling, and be flagged by the commander in accordance with AR 600-8-22.

Overweight soldiers cannot: be promoted, hold command, command sergeant major or first sergeant positions, attend professional military schools, or receive an award.

Weapons

Weapons must be cleared before being handled to avoid accidents, which are a major cause of casualties during combat and training. When firing, soldiers should adhere to the fundamentals of marksmanship: hold a steady position, adjust the sight picture for proper aim, control breathing, and cleanly squeeze trigger. Adjusting the sight picture requires setting the sight alignment and aiming point.

Basic rifle marksmanship encompasses five different phases: preliminary rifle instruction (PRI), downrange feedback, field fire, advanced rifle marksmanship, and advanced optics, laser, and iron sights. The only two positions taught during PRI are individual foxhole (supported) and basic prone (unsupported). Soldiers work with weaponeers to improve their marksmanship and learn the application of misfire procedures.

All soldiers must know how to clean their weapons, clear stoppages, and fix malfunctions. Cleaning weapons requires cleaner, lubricant, and preservative (CLP). Cleaner is a solvent used to dissolve firing residue and carbon. Lubricant dries into Teflon, increasing lubrication while firing. Preservative is used to preserve the gun by preventing rust. Failing to clean weapons properly can cause stoppages.

Stoppages occur when an automatic or semiautomatic firearm doesn't complete its cycle of operation. When a stoppage occurs, soldiers should attempt immediate or remedial action. Immediate actions include initial attempts to resolve the issue and troubleshooting if the issue remains. The Army troubleshoots stoppages based on the acronym SPORTS: slap, pull, observe, release, tap, and shoot. If immediate action fails once, then remedial action must be taken. Remedial action involves continuing to locate the specific issue and making all attempts to clear the stoppage. Malfunctions occur when a severe stoppage causes the weapon to completely stop firing; these typically involve the mechanical failure of a weapon, magazine, or ammo.

Army leaders should be familiar with assembling, cleaning, reloading and firing, identifying stoppages, and taking immediate and remedial actions for a number of weapons. Common weapons used by Army leaders include M2 (.50 caliber machine gun), M4 (5.56 mm semiautomatic rifle), M9 (pistol), M11 (pistol), M16/A2 (5.56 mm semiautomatic rifle), M18A1 (Claymore), M240B (machine gun), M249 (machine gun), M60 (machine gun), M136 AT4 (rocket launcher), M72 (light anti-tank weapon), M203 (40 mm grenade launcher), grenade machine gun, hand grenades, and MK19 (40 mm).

Battle Focused Training

Battle focus is peacetime training that replicates the battlefield by being tough, realistic, and challenging. Leaders of battle focused training exercises practice integrating combat support (CS) and combat service support systems (CSS) to maximize combat power. Battle focused training can occur through demonstration, conference, and lecture. Lecture is the least preferred and demonstration is the most preferred. FM 7-1 governs battle-focused training.

While conducting battle focused training, commanders place an emphasis on avoiding accidents, which account for the most casualties in combat. Risk assessments are used to increase an operation's safety. Battle focused training often occurs at night and under adverse weather conditions to prepare soldiers for success.

Commanders use a Battlefield Operating System (BOS) to organize battle tasks. The lowest level of unit with battle tasks is the battalion. A battle roster is a list of individuals, crews, or elements involved in war fighting. A crew drill allows crews to practice operating their designated weapon or equipment.

Live, virtual, and constructive training is used to achieve and sustain proficiency on Mission Essential Task List (METL). Different types of exercises include Fire Coordination Exercise (FCX), Command Post Exercise (CPX), Command Field Exercise (CFX), Field Training Exercise (FTX), and Situational Training Exercise (STX). In addition, Army leaders conduct Tactical Exercise Without Troops (TEWT) to train officer and NCO battlefield leaders. Battle focused training is also conducted with training aids to enhance learning opportunities. Simulations train leaders how to find alternative ways to maneuver during battle, and simulators replicate all the functions in a given system.

Training the Force

Training involves instructing soldiers so they can reach their potential peak performance at military functions and tasks. Strong soldiers are the Army's foundation, so training is the number one priority. The Army mandates performance-oriented training, allowing soldiers to learn through hands-on experience. Whenever feasible, all Army training is as realistic as possible to strengthen soldiers' confidence and competence in the field. Training policies and procedures are described in FM 7-0.

The Army uses a color-coded **Time Management System** to increase the efficiency of training. Green means training collective tasks during multi-echelon training. Amber means training with a small unit. Red means training with sub-organizations to conduct specialized individual, leader, and crew training.

Commanders hold overall responsibility for training, and NCOs train individuals, small teams, and crews. The objective of training seeks to maintain and sustain proficiency, develop leaders, and practice adapting to conditions. Training is performance oriented, conducted under realistic conditions focused on combat proficiency. In addition, training includes multi-echelon techniques and features combined arms and joint team exercises. Multi-echelon training simultaneously integrates individual and collective tasks at different levels, and it is the most effective and efficient way to train for a Mission Essential Task List (METL).

Commanders develop long-range, short-range, and near-term training plans. In addition, commanders set the operations tempo (OPTEMPO) of an organization, which is used to plan for future fuel and repair costs related to training.

In order to determine proficiency, the Army conducts informal, formal, internal, and external evaluations. Informal evaluations are conducted with a leader who provides immediate feedback. A special evaluator conducts formal evaluations. Internal evaluations are planned, resourced, and conducted by the organization being evaluated. External evaluations are planned, resourced, and conducted by an organization that's higher in the chain of command than the organization being evaluated.

Leaders conduct after-action reviews (AARs) to provide feedback. AARs are to be treated as discussions and learning opportunities, not critiques. They are meant to enhance soldiers' critical learning experiences, including operational, institutional, and self-development domains.

First Aid

First aid is administered to casualties before medical care can be provided. The objective is to prevent the presenting condition to worsen, particularly in life-threatening situations. First aid responders should focus on stopping the bleeding, relieving pain, preventing infection, and overcoming shock. They also use the mnemonic ABC to remember to sustain airways, breathing, and circulation. Self-aid is the same as first aid except it is applied by the casualties to themselves. FM 4-25.11 reviews the Army's first aid procedures.

The pulse can be checked at any of the following arteries: the carotid (neck), femoral (groin), radial (wrist), and posterior tibial (ankle). Cardiopulmonary resuscitation (CPR) is conducted when the casualty has no heartbeat. Rescue breathing can be done mouth to mouth and mouth to nose. The first responder must continue attempts to restore breathing until: a doctor says stop, the casualty starts breathing, someone relieves the first responder, or if the first responder can't physically continue. Unconscious casualties should be left with their head to the side to prevent asphyxiation by vomit.

Shock can be identified based on the following symptoms: blotched skin, clammy skin, confusion, fast breathing, nausea, restlessness, and thirst. Treatment for shock follows the acronym PELCRN (position on back, elevate legs, loosen clothing, climatize, reassure, and notify medical personnel).

Wounds should be dressed and bandaged as soon as possible to control bleeding and prevent contamination. The human body has eleven pressure points, and when pressed, they can be used to control bleeding. A tourniquet should be applied between the wound and heart, not directly over the wound, when the bleeding can't otherwise be controlled.

The Army groups burns into four categories: thermal, electric, chemical, and laser. Burn casualties should first be removed from the source of burn. Medication or cream should never be applied to a burn.

Soldiers suffer three different types of heat injuries: heat cramps, heat exhaustion, and heat stroke. Heat cramps feature excessive sweating and occurs in the arms, legs, and abdomen. Heat exhaustion includes the same symptoms as heat cramps with additional symptoms, including headaches, weakness, dizziness, nausea, confusion, difficulty breathing, tingling, and confusion. Heat stroke is more severe than cramps and exhaustion, and it can result in seizures and unconsciousness.

The Army follows the acronym COLD to protect soldiers from injury caused by cold temperatures. **COLD** stands for clean, overheating avoidance, loose and layered clothing, and dry. Frostbite is first noticeable when skin turns numb with white patches. If frostbite is noticed, the surrounding clothing must be removed and then the frostbite must be warmed with body heat, dressed, and presented to medical personnel.

If a medical evacuation is possible, triage should be conducted, meaning the casualties are sorted into the following evacuation categories: Urgent (within 2 hours), Priority (4 hours), and Routine (24 hours).

Maintenance

The Army Maintenance Management System (TAMMS) is how the Army maximizes efficient use of equipment. Commanders are required to maintain government equipment at the Army Maintenance Standard, meaning that the equipment is operationally ready. Technical manuals (TM) instruct operators on how to repair their equipment. The Army Material Maintenance Policy is covered in AR 750-1, and TAMMS is covered in DA PAM 750-8.

Maintenance Assistance and Instruction (MAIT) teams provide guidance on maintenance programs. Historical records are used to permanently document equipment's operation, maintenance, ownership, and ultimate disposal. For example, DA Form 2408-4 is a historical record for weapons, and DA Form 2408-4 records the ammunition condition report.

Every operator of equipment is required to conduct Preventative Maintenance Checks and Service (PMCS). Operators need to conduct PMCS on a weekly and monthly basis as well as before, during, and after using the equipment. PMCS is based on the TM-10 series operator's manual and recorded with DD Form 314. Soldiers must use DA Form 2407 to request maintenance support, and DA Form 2765 is used to request for issue or turn-in.

Vehicles are subject to an intensive quality maintenance program, featuring various dispatch procedures, for the purpose of maintaining the vehicle and creating an audit trail. First, the dispatcher must be appointed based on orders from DA PAM 738-750. Second, the operator must be specifically assigned to the vehicle and equipment. Third, all equipment must be functional according to TM-10 series manuals. Fourth, a service or AOAP sample cannot be due on a piece of equipment. Fifth, the dispatcher must inspect the operators OF-346. Sixth, the equipment must be suitable for the mission. DA PAM 750-35 governs the Army's motor pool operations.

Supply Economy

The Army categorizes supplies in ten different classes. Class I includes rations. Class II includes clothing and equipment. Class III is fuels and lubricants. Class IV is materials used for fortification. Class V includes ammunition and explosives. Class VI is personal items. Class VII is major end items. Class VIII is medical supplies. Class IX is spare parts for repairs. Class X covers miscellaneous supplies. Some of these items are referred to as Extendable Supplies when they are only capable of being used once, such as rations.

The Army uses the term "supply economy" to refer to the efficient use of supplies. In particular, the Army is seeking to limit waste and abuse. For supply economy, the best rule of thumb is to assess what is required for the given situation and then only use what is necessary. Every individual who handles Army supplies in any capacity is accountable and responsible for maintaining supply economy.

The **Report of Survey** is used in supply economy to assess the loss, damage, or destruction of supplies. The Report of Survey must be commenced within fifteen calendar days after the issue is found, and the initiation process takes 5 days. The investigation begins when DA Form 4697 is submitted to the commanding officer.

When a soldier is found to be responsible for replacing the property, they will receive a Statement of Charges and must pay the total amount. Once a soldier is in the Army for 6 months, they will receive a Clothing Allowance, which is used to replace unserviceable pieces of their uniform and gear. The Clothing Allowance is dispersed on an annual basis on the anniversary of the soldier's enlistment date. Soldiers are not required to use their Clothing Allowance to replace unserviceable clothing when they are not at fault. Under those circumstances, the soldier will receive a Gratuitous Issue, meaning that the lost or destroyed clothing is replaced for free.

The Army establishes responsibility over equipment through receipts. If a soldier signs a hand receipt, then they are directly responsible for that equipment. As such, soldiers have a duty to inspect that the stated equipment is present and in serviceable condition before signing the receipt. Otherwise the soldier is responsible for the discrepancy. The only ways to stop being accountable for an item are through a report of survey, statement of charges, cash collection voucher, or turn-in of the items.

Sample Questions and Answers

1. Who designs the Army's fitness training programs?

Master Fitness Trainers (MFT) are certified trainers, and they design and implement the Army's fitness training programs.

2. What are Class I supplies?

Class I supplies are rations.

3. How does the Department of Defense's weight control standards differ from AR 600-9?

The Department of Defense is a more rigorous weight control standard than AR 600-9. In addition, AR 600-9 is mandatory, while all soldiers are strongly encouraged to strive toward the Department of Defense's goal of 18% body fat for males and 26% body fat for females.

4. What is FM 7-1?

FM 7-1 governs battle focused training.

5. What is the difference between a stoppage and malfunction?

Stoppages occur when a firearm doesn't complete its cycle of operation, while malfunctions cause a weapon to completely stop firing. Furthermore, stoppages usually result from a failure to sufficiently clean the weapon, while malfunctions often involve a mechanical failure.

6. What type of weapon is the M72?

The M72 is a light anti-tank weapon.

7. What does "O" stand for in the acronym SPORTS?

"O" stands for observe in the acronym SPORTS, which stands for ways to troubleshoot stoppages in weapons.

8. What type of weapon is the M18A1?

M18A1 is a Claymore mine.

9. How does a soldier add a layer of Teflon to a weapon?

Soldiers can add a layer of Teflon by using lubricant during the cleaning process.

10. What should be done if dressing the wound doesn't stop the bleeding?

If bleeding can't be controlled, the soldier administering first aid should apply a tourniquet between the wound and heart.

11. What is generally the shortest phase of physical fitness?

The preparatory phase is the shortest phase of physical fitness. This phase lasts for 2 weeks. In contrast, the conditioning and maintenance phases are indefinite, and they last until the soldier meets all their fitness-related goals for the mission.

12. How long is the timeframe for a Priority medical evacuation?

Priority designation means the casualty must be evacuated within 4 hours. A Priority medical evacuation is the middle ground between the Urgent (within 2 hours) and Routine (24 hours) evacuation categories.

13. Other than preparing soldiers for combat, what is the purpose of the Army Weight Control Program?

The Army Weight Control Program's secondary purpose is to ensure that all soldiers have a proper military appearance.

14. What is the most serious heat-related injury?

Heat stroke can result in seizures and unconsciousness, making it more severe than heat cramps and heat exhaustion; however, if left untreated, heat cramps and heat exhaustion can lead to a heat stroke.

15. How do commanders estimate future fuel and repair costs related to training?

Commanders estimate future fuel and repair costs related to training based on the battalion's OPTEMPO.

16. What is a Statement of Charges?

Soldiers receive a Statement of Charges when they are found responsible for damage or destruction to government property and must pay to replace it.

17. What are the Army's four fitness tasks?

The Army's fitness tasks are classified as collective tasks, individual tasks, leader tasks, and resources for training.

18. What is the most effective way to train for a METL?

Multi-echelon training is the most effective and efficient way to train for a Mission Essential Task List (METL). This style of training simultaneously integrates individual and collective tasks at different organizational levels.

19. Why is it so important to inspect materials before signing a hand receipt?

Soldiers are directly responsible for property once they sign a hand receipt, so they must inspect the property to ensure it is present and serviceable. If a soldier fails to inspect the property that's already damaged before signing the hand receipt, then they are held responsible for the discrepancy.

20. What is the red phase in the Army's Time Management System?

In the Army's Time Management System, red means training with sub-organizations to conduct specialized individual, leader, and crew training.

21. How is clothing replaced when the owner is not at fault?

If the owner of the clothing is not at fault for the damage, the clothing is by Gratuitous Issue, which doesn't count against the soldier's Clothing Allowance.

22. What is FM 21-20?

FM 21-20 governs physical fitness training.

23. What does the letter L stand for in COLD?

The letter L stands for loose and layered clothing in COLD, which is an acronym used to protect soldiers from the cold.

24. What needs to happen before a vehicle can be dispatched?

First, the dispatcher must be appointed based on orders from DA PAM 738-750. Second, the operator must be specifically assigned to the vehicle and equipment. Third, all equipment must be functional according to TM-10 series manuals. Fourth, a service or AOAP sample cannot be due on a piece of equipment. Fifth, the dispatcher must inspect the operators OF-346. Sixth, the equipment must be suitable for the mission.

25. How does the Army Maintenance Management System (TAMMS) use historical records?

Historical records are part of the Army Maintenance Management System (TAMMS), and they are used to permanently document equipment's operation, maintenance, ownership, and ultimate disposal.

26. What is the purpose of battle focused training?

Battle focus training seeks to prepare soldiers for war by replicating battlefield conditions. As a result, battle focused training is tough, realistic, and challenging. In addition, battle focused training often occurs at night and under adverse weather conditions to prepare soldiers for success.

27. What is DA Form 4697?

The submission of DA Form 4697 to a commanding officer begins a Report of Survey, which is an investigation to assess the loss, damage, or destruction of supplies. DA Form 4697 must be commenced within fifteen calendar days after the issue is discovered.

28. What type of weapon is the M203?

M203 is a 40-mm grenade launcher.

29. What is the first step in treating frostbite?

The surrounding clothing must be removed before the frostbite is warmed with body heat, dressed, and presented to medical personnel.

30. How is a tape test conducted?

To conduct a tape test, two soldiers use a non-stretchable tape measure to measure a soldier's body fat. Men are measured at the abdomen and neck, and women are measured at the neck, waist, and hip.

31. What is AR 750-1?

AR 750-1 expresses the Army Material Maintenance Policy.

32. What is the purpose of TAMMS?

The Army Maintenance Management System (TAMMS) aims to maximize efficient use of equipment.

33. What is the least preferred method of battle focused training?

The least preferred method of battle focused training is by lecture.

34. What is the longest interval a soldier can go between weigh-ins?

Soldiers must be weighed every 6 months.

35. Which type of battle focused training exercise is specifically focused on training officers and NCOs?

Tactical Exercise Without Troops (TEWT) is conducted specifically to train officer and NCOs.

36. What does "P" stand for in the acronym PELCRN?

"P" stands for position on back in the acronym PELCRN, which is a first aid treatment for shock.

37. What is the alternate APFT?

The alternate Army Physical Fitness Test (APFT) is available for soldiers who are 55 or older, and it includes push-ups, sit-ups, and an aerobic event.

38. What is the purpose of an AAR?

Leaders conduct after-action reviews (AARs) to discuss the mission, provide feedback, and enhance soldiers' critical learning experiences, including operational, institutional, and self-development domains.

39. How can a soldier prevent stoppages?

Soldiers can prevent stoppages by following the acronym CLP, which stands for cleaner, lubricant, and preservative. Cleaner is a solvent used to dissolve firing residue and carbon. Lubricant dries into Teflon, increasing lubrication while firing. Preservative is used to preserve the gun by preventing rust.

40. What tool does the Army use to identify soldiers at risk of violating AR 600-9?

Weight-screening tables are used to determine if a soldier is at risk of violating AR-600-9, which defines the Army's standards for body fat.

Operations

Army Plan

The **Army Strategic Campaign Plan** places the highest priority on defending the homeland from attack. To accomplish this goal, the Army pursues two strategic objectives. First, the Army will have fully trained and equipped soldiers led by advanced leaders. Second, the Army will have the capability to deploy relevant and ready land power as part of the Joint Team.

Army training seeks to produce soldiers with a mastery of critical steps in a range of military operations. Army training initiatives include implementing homeland defensive postures, increasing proficiency against irregular challenges, improving stability operations and strategic responsiveness, fighting in complex terrain, bolstering global force posture, strengthening battle command, and enhancing Joint Force capability, including logistics.

The **Rapid Fielding Initiative** is an Army initiative dedicated to providing soldiers with the most advanced and effective equipment. Technology plays a critical role in modern combat operations, especially in terms of integrating constant, effective, and timely logistical support.

In addition to fully training and equipping troops, the Army emphasizes soldiers' adaptability. The modern war-fighting environment demands that soldiers be capable of reacting to rapid changes and adjusting approaches to fit recent developments on the ground. In addition, soldiers must be capable of shaping the environment itself to maximize their advantages.

Land Navigation and Map Reading

Maps use symbols to represent the Earth's surface and features within four quadrants (northeast, southeast, northwest, and southwest). Maps have numerous strategic military applications for senior leadership, and soldiers can use maps to calculate accurate distances, find locations, and identify optimal travel routes. FM 2-35.6 reviews map reading and land navigation tactics.

The United States uses the Universal Transverse Mercator (UTM) map system. This system categorizes maps based on the size of the scale. The scale can usually be found in the Legend on the map's lower left side. Small-scale maps have a scale of 1:1,000,000 or smaller, covering large areas with minimal detail, and it is mostly used for general planning. Medium-scale maps have a scale between 1:1,000,000 and 1:75,000, but the most commonly used scale for medium-scale maps is 1:250,000. This type of map is typically used for operational planning since it covers a fairly large area in moderate detail. Large-scale maps have a scale that's at least 1:75,000, but the most commonly used scale is 1:50,000. Enlisted soldiers and junior leaders most often use large-scale maps.

Prior to use, soldiers must orient the map by using a compass or terrain association. Maps often include parallels of latitude and longitude, which create a grid for soldiers to find exact locations. Latitude lines run east to west and measure a position's distance from the Equator. Longitude lines run north to south and measure a position's distance from the Prime Meridian. Both lines of latitude and longitude are measured in degrees, and one degree covers 17.7 mils.

Military maps display grid north, magnetic north, and true north. When soldiers use a compass with the map, magnetic north is used but otherwise grid north is most often used. Soldiers need to find at least two known locations on the map and ground to accurately plot their current location.

Topographic maps are used to depict terrain and land forms, including their horizontal features. These maps have index, intermediary, and supplementary contour lines, which are used to measure elevation. Contour intervals can be used to determine if a slope is gentle, steep, concave, or convex.

Symbols on topographic maps are not drawn to scale, and they represent man-made and natural features. Natural features are categorized as major, minor, and supplementary features. Examples of major terrain features include hills, ridges, valleys, saddles, and depressions. Examples of minor terrain features include draws, spurs, and cliffs. Examples of supplementary features include cuts and fills.

A compass has two sights and two scales (degrees and mils), and it always points to magnetic north. Soldiers use either the compass-to-cheek method or center-hold method. Lensatic compasses need to be held firm, level, and away from metal, and they have luminous dials and needles for night use.

Chemical, Biological, Radiological, Nuclear

The Army categorizes the hazards of nuclear, biological, and chemical (NBC) contamination as either immediate or residual. Immediate hazards produce casualties in the attack's immediate aftermath, while residual hazards are delayed and generally longer term. The Army uses audible alarms, automatic alarms, and virtual signals to warn soldiers about NBC. If forced to pass through contamination, soldiers must try not to stir dust or touch anything that is potentially contaminated. FM 3-11 reviews NBC operations.

Once a soldier identifies NBC contamination, they should immediately stop breathing, close eyes, place protective mask on head, clear mask, check seal, sound alarm, and then continue mission. Masks don't protect against ammonia vapors or carbon monoxide poisoning. Only the commander can order the unit to unmask. FM 3-11.4 describes NBC protection procedures. Decontamination is immediate, operational, and thorough. FM 3-5 reviews NBC decontamination procedures.

Nuclear bursts can be deployed over the air, on the ground, or under the surface with the airburst being the most powerful. Any nuclear burst creates devastating heat and radiation explosions. The initial blast is the most dangerous part of a nuclear attack, but the radiation also causes long-term damage to the surrounding area. Unlike chemical and biological weapons, the United States reserves the right to use nuclear weapons preemptively if deemed necessary to America's national security interests. The authority to launch nuclear weapons lies solely with the president of the United States, and it has happened once in American history. President Harry S. Truman authorized the use of atomic weapons to avoid a costly invasion of Japan in the process and effectively end World War II.

Biological weapons intentionally contaminate an enemy with germs or toxins to cause death and destruction. Bacteria, fungi, rickettsia, and viruses can all be used as biological agents. Biological warfare would most likely target cities, large military installations, and food sources. The United States follows a policy of no use for biological weapons.

Chemical agents can be deployed with arterial sprays, bombs, mines, and rockets. Examples of chemical agents that can be used as weapons include nerve, blister, blood, and choking gases. Of those chemicals, the nerve agent is the deadliest. The US categorizes chemical agents as persistent, non-persistent, or dusty. Chemical attacks are most effective when there's less wind and sun, so chemical attacks are most often launched during the morning and evening. The US follows a policy of No First Use, meaning that the United States will use chemical weapons if attacked with chemical weapons first.

Radiological warfare means inflicting radiation poisoning on enemies, typically through a nuclear explosion. These types of weapons release radioactive materials into the environment, and the materials can enter the body in a variety of ways, including absorption, inhalation, and ingestion. Signs of radiation poisoning may be delayed, appearing several hours after the exposure, and the relevant symptoms include nausea, vomiting, diarrhea, and burns. The United States imposes extensive protections to secure its own proprietary radioactive material to secure and prevent accidental exposure. In addition, the military prioritizes denying rogue states, terrorists, and other malign actors from accessing radioactive material to make a dirty bomb.

Field Sanitation

Field sanitation involves creating and maintaining a healthy environment in the field by controlling disposing waste (human, liquid, garbage, and rubbish). The Army improves field sanitation by making sure soldiers are aware of the five "F"s: fingers, feces, flies, food, and fluids. FM 21-10 reviews field hygiene and sanitation procedures, and FM 4-25.12 governs the field sanitation team.

The Army prevents the spread of communicable diseases by controlling and eliminating vectors. The Army has five categories of communicable diseases: respiratory, intestinal, insect-borne, venereal, and miscellaneous. Common vectors for communicable diseases include insects and rodents. For example, flies can carry typhoid, and mosquitos can carry malaria.

Safeguarding water is critical to field sanitation. The goal is to have water that's both palatable and potable. **Palatable water** tastes pleasant, but it might be unsafe. In contrast, **potable water** is safe, but it might taste unpleasant. Water can be purified with iodine tablets or boiling. If untreated, water can spread bacillary diseases like cholera, diarrhea, dysentery, leptospirosis, and typhoid. Soldiers in the field should conserve water, avoid contamination, and drink only water that has been approved by medical personnel. A Lister bag holds 36 gallons of water, and people in temperate zones should drink 5 gallons of water per day.

Human waste can be disposed with borehole latrines, burnout latrines, mound latrines, pail latrines, cat holes, deep pits, straddle trenches, and urine soak pits. Latrines should never be located within 100 feet of a water source, and they should always be located 100 meters downhill or downstream from the mess hall. Nonhuman waste should be disposed of in garbage pits, which cannot be located within 30 yards of a mess area or 100 feet from water sources.

Physical Security

Physical security is a critical part of **Operations Security (OPSEC)**. The goal of physical security is to prevent and protect against unauthorized use and enemy action taken against equipment, and property. Important aspects of physical security include controlling population, achieving information dominance, and implementing anti-terrorism measures. Physical security also includes the deployment of physical security equipment as a force multiplier and the integration of multinational and interagency assets. FM 3-19.30 reviews the Army's physical security policies and procedures.

The Army Physical Security Program is designed to inform all personnel with physical security measures to increase its efficiency and effectiveness. The program seeks to keep personnel safe, stop unauthorized access to intelligence, and protect against espionage, sabotage, damage, and theft. AR 190-13 governs the Army Physical Security Program.

Physical plans aim to detect, delay, and respond to threats in a variety of ways. An installation's physical plan typically includes general and special guard orders, lighting systems, access control, material control, locks, identification system, and protective barriers. The physical plan should be careful to identify and plug all potential gaps in the protection, which are referred to as vulnerabilities.

Facilities, classified material, and property are protected with locks. As such, every container, room, and facility is kept locked when unused. If security lighting is unavailable, physical plans call for additional security posts, patrols, military working dog (MWD) patrols, and use of night vision devices (NVDs).

The Army classifies restricted areas as controlled areas (least secure), limited areas, and exclusion areas (most secure). Protective barriers are used to limit entry into restricted areas and to designate their boundaries. These are similar to the protective barriers that surround military installations. Examples of protective barriers include chain link fences, barbed wire, and concrete barriers. Restricted areas also have signs displaying the conditions for entry placed at least 50-feet from the point of entry.

Security and Intelligence

Operations Security (OPSEC) is undertaken to prevent enemies and potential enemies from gathering information about the Army's intentions, plans, and operations. The Army is particularly interested in protecting information related to size, activity, location, uniform, time, and equipment (SALUTE). AR 380-5 governs security procedures.

The Army protects intelligence through a security classification system. From most secure to least, the classifications are Top Secret, Secret, and Confidential. Every document has a single classification. Even with a proper clearance, access can still be denied because information is provided on a need to know basis. Top Secret material must be destroyed through burning or pulping.

Counterintelligence seeks to thwart Subversion and Espionage Direction Against the Army (SAEDA). For example, using a challenge and password that changes every 24 hours is a counterintelligence tactic. The Army also uses technology to protect against and conduct meaconing, intrusion, jamming, and interference (MIJI).

When gathering intelligence from POWs, the Army follows the 5 S's: search, segregate, silence, speed, and safeguard. POWs should be grouped into officers, NCOs, privates, deserters, females, civilians, and political staff.

Guard Duty

The commander of the guard is responsible for instructing, disciplining, and supervising guards. The duties of a guard include memorizing, interpreting, and complying with general and special orders, including the countersign and parole word. Guard duty typically lasts for 2 to 4 hours. The automatic punishment for sleeping on guard duty is court-martial. When indoors, guards are required to salute unless otherwise engaged in a specific duty that prevents saluting. FM 22-6 governs guard duty.

FM 22-6 contains the guard's three general orders. First, guards are responsible for everything within limits of post and can quit only after being properly relieved. Second, guards will obey special orders and perform all duties in a military manner. Third, guards will report violations of special orders, emergencies, and anything else not already in the instructions left for the commander of the relief. In contrast, the post commander issues special orders to tell guards exactly what to do. Special orders define the countersign (challenge and password) and when to issue challenges. During the inspection, guard inspectors use the parole word to check the countersign. Article 101 of the UCMJ prescribes death or other such punishment as decided by court-martial for soldiers who unlawfully disclose the parole word or countersign. Rifles should be held at post arms while challenging, and vehicles are challenged the same as people on foot, except the driver and/or passenger can be ordered out of the vehicle. When challenging, guards must use only the minimum amount of force needed to apprehend the individuals.

The Army classified guards as interior or exterior. Interior guards patrol the inside of military installations to protect Army property, and they're usually required to strictly follow the general orders. The interior guards who patrol a fixed area are called the main guards, and interior guards who protect sensitive areas of the installation are called special guards. Exterior guards patrol outside of a military installation, and they are primarily used in combat areas or hostile territory. Examples of exterior guards include lookouts, listening posts, and outposts. Compared to interior guards, exterior guards have significantly more leeway, and they're usually only bound by special orders.

Desert Operations

Deserts are difficult terrain due to the lack of water, extreme heat, and lack of concealment. For example, desert temperatures have reached a high of 136 degrees Fahrenheit. As such, the Army prioritizes adapting to the terrain and climate. FM 90-3 reviews procedures and tactics for conducting desert operations.

There are three distinct types of desert. First, **mountain deserts** have a scattering of barren hills or mountains with dry basins in between. Second, **rocky plateau deserts** are mostly flat with some large rocks on the surface. Third, **sandy (dune) deserts** are large stretches of flat areas composed of sand or gravel.

The desert environment is hazard to military equipment. Adverse terrain features include heat, humidity, wind, dust, sand, temperature swings, thermal and optical bending, and radiant light. For example, the desert climate causes technological issues with radios due to overheating. Radio equipment must be kept as cool as possible, requiring soldiers to keep it out of direct sunlight, using it on low power, using wet rags, creating shade, and leaving vents open.

Soldiers can develop **agoraphobia**, the fear of open spaces, after conducting operations without any natural cover. Other common desert diseases include malaria, dengue fever, dysentery, cholera, and typhoid.

Army leaders must monitor troops' hydration levels while operating in the desert. A lack of alertness is an early warning sign, and urine is the strongest indicator for hydration. Dehydration can cause numerous health issues, like constipation, hemorrhoids, kidney stones, and urinary tract infections. As such, soldiers must be told to drink before they become thirsty, carry at least one extra canteen of water in reserve, and know where water can be located. If a soldier fears they're dehydrated, they should stop working, rest in the shade, and rehydrate.

Water should be stored in plastic cans or coolers whenever possible because water in plastic cans lasts seventy-two hours, while water in metal containers lasts 24 hours. If the water trailers remain cool, the water is safe for approximately 5 days. Ice should be removed from a water trailer before moving it. During missions, the water containers should be well protected and easily dismounted. Water that becomes unusable can be used on clothing to keep cool.

Survival

The Army uses the acronym SURVIVAL to summarize its survival concepts. Soldiers should size up the situation, use all five senses, remember where they are, vanquish fear and panic, improvise as necessary, value staying alive, act like the area's native people, and live by their wits. Soldiers can help avoid detection by identifying the enemy's capabilities, deploying countermeasures, applying camouflage, minimizing movement, using decoys, and avoiding operational patterns. FM 3-05.70 reviews the policies and procedures for survival situations.

Survival situations can cause soldiers to feel a range of emotions, including anger, boredom, fear, frustration, loneliness, and stress. These emotions are natural and cannot be entirely eliminated; instead, soldiers should manage their emotions and embrace possible benefits. For example, stress allows people to sharpen their focus, strengths, and values.

The basic needs for staying healthy are food, water, hygiene, rest, and immunizations. During survival situations, acquiring a safe water supply is the most important need to stay healthy. Whenever the temperature exceeds 100 degrees Fahrenheit, soldiers should drink one quart of water per hour, and at all other times in arid areas, soldiers should drink one pint per hour.

While operating in arid waters, soldiers must be cognizant that food, water, cover, and shelter are in limited supply. In addition, physical movement is demanding, and land navigation is difficult. Wild animals and natural sources of water might not always be safe. The taste of wild plants can be improved through soaking, boiling, cooking, and leaching. Soldiers in the wilderness should avoid poisonous plants, such as poison ivy, poison oak, and poison sumac.

To evade enemies, soldiers should find a hide site in accordance with the acronym BLISS. The hide site should: blend with surrounding, low in silhouette, irregular in shape, small in size, and secluded. Existing buildings or shelters shouldn't be considered as a hide site. If a platoon member is not involved in building the hide site or other defensive position, they should be providing security. Once the hide site is erected, soldiers should implement a patrol for the purpose of gathering intelligence.

When a unit is dispersed, soldiers should make their way to the rally point. If the soldier sees an overhead flare, they should immediately get low and stop all movements. In survival situations, traveling at night is safer than traveling in daylight. It takes the eyes approximately 30 minutes to develop natural night vision. If an area's concealment is limited and enemy fire prevents the soldier from standing upright, they should move in the low-crawl position. Contact with friendlies should be made only when there is enough light to make an identification.

Camouflage, Concealment, and Decoys

Camouflage, Concealment, and Decoys (CCD) involves using materials and techniques to prevent detection of activities, installation, personnel, troop movements, and equipment. The best way to prevent detection is to hide, blend, disguise, decoy, or disrupt appearances with the aid of environmental, natural, and artificial materials. Every soldier is individually responsible for CCD, and FM 20-3 reviews these tactics.

Applying camouflage to fighting and hiding positions helps them blend into the background. Camouflaged should be applied during the position's preparation. Soldiers should also be cognizant of how activity disturbs natural terrain patterns, including agricultural, urban, wooded, barren, and arctic terrain. For example, if soldiers need to gather materials for the position, they should be common to the area but taken from as far away as possible. Similarly, excess dirt from digging the position should be taken to the rear, and any tracks that lead to the position must be covered or brushed away. Once the position is complete, the soldier should inspect it from at least 35 meters away from the enemy's perspective. The position's camouflage should be altered if it doesn't look natural and blend into the surrounding area.

Cover is physical protection from bullets, projectiles, flames, and NBC agents, and concealment is protection from enemy observation. Cover and concealment can either be natural or artificial. Natural cover and concealment examples include bushes, grass, ravines, shadows, and trees. Artificial examples include foxholes, trenches, and walls. Decoys are false targets that attract the enemy's attention, and soldiers use them to draw fire away from actual targets.

Sample Questions and Answers

1. What is the UTM?

The Universal Transverse Mercator (UTM) is the map system used by the United States military, and it categorizes maps based on the size of the scale.

2. What is FM 3-11?

FM 3-11 governs nuclear, biological, and chemical (NBC) operations.

3. What is the purpose of OPSEC?

Operations Security (OPSEC) is undertaken to prevent enemies and potential enemies from gathering information about the Army's intentions, plans, and operations.

4. What is the difference between general and special orders?

The three general orders apply to every guard, and special orders tell guards exactly what to do.

5. What is the Rapid Fielding Initiative?

The Rapid Fielding Initiative is an Army initiative dedicated to providing soldiers with the most advanced and effective equipment.

6. What characteristics make deserts difficult terrain to operate in?

Deserts are difficult terrain due to the lack of water, extreme heat and humidity, wind, dust, sand, thermal and optical blending, radiant light, and the lack of concealment.

7. What does the "U" in SURVIVAL stand for?

The "U" in the SURVIVAL acronym stands for "Use all five senses."

8. What is the purpose of camouflage?

The purpose of camouflage is to blend equipment, troops, and fighting and hiding positions into the background.

9. How much water should a soldier keep in reserve while operating in the desert?

Soldiers should carry at least one extra canteen of water in reserve while operating in the desert.

10. How do soldiers plot their current location on a map?

Soldiers plot their current location on a map by matching two locations on the ground with their corresponding locations on the map.

11. Where should soldiers gather materials for a hiding position?

Materials should be gathered from as far away as possible to avoid disturbing the natural terrain patterns and disrupting the camouflage.

12. How does the Army categorize natural terrain features?

The Army categorizes natural terrain features as major, minor, and supplementary.

13. What type of navigation device has luminous dials and needles?

Lensatic compasses have luminous dials and needles.

14. What type of material is best for storing water?

Water should be stored in plastic containers because it lasts 48 hours longer than water stored in metal containers.

15. What is a protective barrier?

Protective barriers are used to limit entry into restricted areas and to designate their boundaries. Examples include chain link fences, barbed wire, and concrete barriers.

16. Why does the Army emphasize adaptability during training?

The Army emphasizes adaptability during training because the modern war-fighting environment demands that soldiers be capable of reacting to rapid changes, adjusting approaches to fit recent developments on the ground, and shaping the environment itself to maximize their advantages.

17. What is the least secure type of classified intelligence?

The least secure type of classified intelligence is marked Confidential.

18. What is FM 4-25.12?

FM 4-25.12 directs the field sanitation team.

19. What are the steps a soldier must take after identifying NBC contamination?

Once a soldier identifies NBC contamination, they should immediately stop breathing, close eyes, place protective mask on head, clear mask, check seal, sound alarm, and then continue mission.

20. What orders are used to issue the countersign?

Special orders define the countersign (challenge and password) and when to issue challenges.

21. How does the United States' policy toward nuclear weapons differ from chemical weapons and biological weapons?

Unlike its policy for chemical weapons and biological weapons, the United States reserves the right to use nuclear weapons preemptively if its national security is threatened.

22. What is the final step for camouflaging a fighting or hiding position?

After completing the position, the soldier should inspect it from at least 35 meters away from the enemy's perspective, and the camouflage should be altered if it doesn't look natural and blend into the surrounding area.

23. How do topographic maps differ from a standard map?

Unlike standard maps, topographic maps contain contour lines to depict the elevation of terrain features.

24. What is FM 3-05.70?

FM 3-05.70 reviews the policies and procedures to be used during survival situations.

25. What is the punishment for unauthorized disclosure of the parole word?

According to Article 101 of the UCMJ, the punishment for unauthorized disclosure of the parole word is death or other such punishment as decided by court-martial.

26. What type of terrain is mostly flat with some large rocks on the surface?

Rocky plateau deserts are mostly flat with some large rocks on the surface.

27. Where does the Army use exterior guards?

Exterior guards are primarily used in combat areas or hostile territory. Examples of exterior guards include lookouts, listening posts, and outposts.

28. What is the range of the scale on a medium-scale map?

Medium-scale maps have a scale between 1:1,000,000 and 1:75,000.

29. What is FM 90-3?

FM 90-3 reviews procedures and tactics for conducting desert operations.

30. What is the importance of locks in a physical security plan?

Locks protect facilities, classified material, and property when they are not actively being used.

31. What is AR 190-13?

AR 190-13 governs the Army Physical Security Program.

32. How does the Army warn soldiers about NBC contamination?

The Army uses audible alarm, automatic alarms, and virtual signals to warn about NBC contamination.

33. What is the difference between lines of longitude and latitude?

Latitude lines run east to west and measure a position's distance from the Equator. In contrast, longitude lines run north to south and measure a position's distance from the Prime Meridian.

34. What could happen if water is left untreated?

If untreated, water can spread bacillary diseases like cholera, diarrhea, dysentery, leptospirosis, and typhoid.

35. How does the Army dispose of nonhuman waste?

Nonhuman waste should be disposed of in garbage pits, which cannot be located within 30 yards of a mess area or 100 feet from water sources.

36. Who is the only person to order a nuclear strike in American history?

President Harry S. Truman ordered a nuclear strike on Japan during World War II, making him the only president to have done so. Atomic bombs were dropped on Hiroshima and Nagasaki on August 6 and August 9, 1945, respectively.

37. What type of guard is a lookout?

Lookouts are exterior guards, and they are primarily used in tactical environments.

38. How are significant amounts of water transported through desert terrain?

Significant amounts of water are transported through desert terrain in water trailer, and any ice should be removed before moving the trailer.

39. What is an MWD patrol?

Military working dog patrols are used to increase visual capabilities when sufficient security lighting cannot be provided.

40. What is the difference between concealment and decoying?

Cover and concealment can either be natural or artificial. Natural cover and concealment examples include bushes, grass, ravines, shadows, and trees. Artificial examples include foxholes, trenches, and walls.

Concealment allows soldiers to camouflage themselves in the environment, increasing their capacity to hide or fight. Decoys are false targets that attract the enemy's attention, and soldiers use them to draw fire away from actual targets.

41. What are symptoms of radiation poisoning?

Symptoms of radiation poisoning include nausea, vomiting, diarrhea, and burns, and they may first appear hours after exposure.

42. What is BLISS?

BLISS is an acronym that stands for the procedures soldiers need to follow when constructing a hiding position. The letters stand for blend with surrounding, low in silhouette, irregular in shape, small in size, and secluded.

43. While operating in an arid area, how much water should a soldier drink when the temperature is below 100 degrees Fahrenheit?

While operating in an arid area with a temperature below 100 degrees Fahrenheit, soldiers should drink one pint of water per hour.

44. Enlisted soldiers and junior leaders most often use what type of map?

Enlisted soldiers and junior leaders most often use large-scale maps with a scale of 1:50,000.

45. What is the benefit of stress in survival situations?

Stress allows people to sharpen their focus, strengths, and values during survival situations.

46. What conditions maximize the impact of chemical weapons?

Lack of wind and sun maximizes the impact of chemical weapons, which is why chemical attacks most often occur during the evening and morning.

47. Why do some soldiers develop agoraphobia?

Soldiers can develop agoraphobia, the fear of open spaces, when operating in the desert because natural concealment is limited.

48. How far must latrines and garbage pits be located from water sources?

Latrines and garbage pits should never be located within 100 feet of a water source.

49. Who is at the top of the chain of command for a guard?

The commander of the relief is at the top of a guard's chain of command.

50. How does the Army Strategic Campaign Plan defend the homeland from attack?

The Army Strategic Campaign Plan defends the homeland from attack by pursuing two strategic objectives. First, the Army will have fully trained and equipped soldiers led by advanced leaders. Second, the Army will have the capability to deploy relevant and ready land power as part of the Joint Team.

Customs

Customs and Courtesies

Installation commanders decide when reveille and retreat sound. Reveille announces the start of the day, and retreat signals the end of the day. The flag is raised when reveille begins, and at the end of retreat, a gun is fired to commence the lowering of the flag. The National Anthem or "To The Color" is played as the flag is lowered, and soldiers must stand at attention and pay the same respect to the flag.

During the days of the Continental Army, soldiers saluted by removing their hat, but it has since evolved into the hand salute. The Army always requires soldiers to salute at indoor ceremonies, during indoor sentry duty, and when reporting to a senior officer. There are four exceptions to the saluting requirement. First, saluting is not required when either the officer or the subordinate is dressed as a civilian. Second, saluting is never required when doing so would significantly disrupt a task or threaten a soldier's safety. Third, soldiers standing in the ranks of a formation are not required to salute. Fourth, saluting is not required in public places, such as a movie theater or grocery store. AR 600-25 governs saluting procedures.

When reporting to an officer at their office, the soldier removes headgear, knocks, and enters only after the officer answers affirmatively. The soldier then approaches the officer's desk, halts, salutes, and says "Sir, ___ reports." The reporting soldier drops the salute only after the officer returns it. After the meeting is over, the soldier salutes, waits until the officer returns the salute, executes facing movement, and departs. The procedure is the same for anywhere else indoors except when the soldier is carrying a weapon in a slip, holster, or by hand (under arms). In that scenario, the salute is altered for the weapon as prescribed and headgear isn't removed. Saluting outdoors is the same as indoors except the soldier directly approaches the officer and halts 3 steps away. If soldiers are in a group and in a situation that requires a salute, the first soldier to see the officer should call the group to attention and collectively salute.

When walking with a senior soldier, the subordinate soldier should walk on the senior soldier's left. Military vehicles are exited in order of seniority. Prisoners are never entitled to salute because they have lost that right.

The Army's official song is "The Army Goes Rolling Along," and it was dedicated on November 11, 1956 (Veteran's Day). The song is played at the end of reviews, parades, and honor guard ceremonies. For the entirety of the song, every soldier must stand and sing all the lyrics.

Flags

The **American flag** is red, white, and blue, with thirteen stripes and fifty stars. Red symbolizes hardiness and valor; white symbolizes purity and innocence; and blue symbolizes vigilance, perseverance, and justice. The thirteen stripes represent the original Thirteen Colonies, and the fifty stars represent the current number of states. After a state enters the Union, a new star is added on the next Fourth of July.

As of January 1966, only five locations have specific legal authority to fly the American flag: United States Capitol, Fort McHenry, Flag House Square, Francis Scott Keys' Grave, and the World War Memorial (Worcester, Massachusetts). The American flag can be displayed flat or hanging free, and when folded properly, it looks like a cocked hat. The flag is never dipped as a salute except when friendly ships of war meet at sea. When military personnel die, the postmaster general presents the flag to the deceased's beneficiary. When the flag is worn out, the stars are cut from it and then the two sections are burned together.

The Army flies five different types of United States flags: Garrison, Post, Field, Storm, and Interment flags. The command sergeant major is typically responsible for safeguarding, caring, and displaying the colors.

Army flagpoles are 50, 60, or 75 feet high, and Building Number 1 can be found at the base of the flagpole at every military post. Flags raised to half-staff must be first briefly raised all the way to the top and only then lowered. AR 600-25 and AR 840-10 cover the procedures for raising and lowering flags.

The **Army flag** features campaign streamers that are 2 ¾ inches wide and 4 feet long. Campaign streamers display the name, commencement date, and end date of each campaign. Current campaigns only have the name and commencement date since they're ongoing. The Army added sixteen campaign streamers during the Revolutionary War with the last streamer reading "Yorktown 28 September–19 October 1781."

Drill and Ceremony

Drill trains soldiers in discipline, precision, and responsiveness to command. In addition, it improves officers and NCOs command over troops. As a result, drill enables troops to be relocated efficiently. The Army teaches drill in the following manners: step-by-step, by the numbers, and talk-through method. The Army holds ceremonies to render honors, uphold traditions, and increase Esprit de Corps. One of the most important Army ceremonies is the review, which is conducted to honor very important guests, present decorations, honor units, and commemorate events. Drill and ceremony are covered in FM 3-2.15.

Soldiers are arranged in either the line or column formation during drill and ceremony. Within formations, a rank is a line with one element in depth, and a file is a column with a single element at the front. An element can be an individual, squad, company, or any other unit of troops.

Soldiers must lead with their left foot, measure steps from heel to heel, and follow the cadence during marches. The cadence is 120 steps per minute for quick time, and 180 steps per minute for double time. The platoon guide controls the direction and rate of march, and they are the only soldier allowed to ever be out of step. Following the halt, there are four rest commands: parade rest, stand at ease, at ease, and rest. "Rear march" is the command used to reverse the unit's direction.

Commands contain a preparatory and execution command, and there is one step or one count in between. There are four different types of commands: two-part, combined, supplementing, and directive. A command cannot be altered once the command of execution has been issued.

Uniforms

Soldiers must never wear the uniform when prohibited by Army regulation and when doing so could potentially discredit the Army. Specifically, the Army prohibits wearing uniforms to support political, commercial, or extremist events. For example, uniforms cannot be worn at public speeches, interviews, picket lines, demonstrations, and during off-duty employment as a civilian unless the soldier receives permission from a competent authority.

When soldiers are outdoors, headgear is a required piece of the Army uniform unless it interferes with safely operating a military vehicle or the soldier is using private or civilian transportation. When indoors, headgear is never worn unless under arms in official capacity or directed to by the commander. Headgear is not required at post-Retreat evening social events when wearing the Army blue and white uniform, enlisted green-dress uniform, or mess uniforms. Commercial headgear is never allowed except when operating motorcycles and other similar vehicles.

Berets are formed to the soldier's head, so the Army prohibits any hairstyle that interferes with the beret's placement. The beret is worn by placing the headband straight across forehead, positioned 1 inch above the soldier's eyebrows. The beret's flash needs to be above the left eye, and the excess material is draped over the right ear, covering no more than half of the ear.

Corporals through sergeant majors and all officers wear ranks and should boards with their uniforms. Soldiers must wear identification tags in aircrafts, during field training, after receiving a commander's directive, and outside the continental United States (OCONUS).

For both the Army Green Service Uniform (Class A) and Army Blue Service Uniform (BDU), the uniform nameplate is 1 x 3 x 1/16-inches and each service stripe represents 3 years of service. When soldiers enter the NCO Corps, headgear changes from beret to service cap and a gold stripe is added to the BDU.

The Army Combat Uniform (ACU) is intended to last for 6 months, and it features a digitized pattern that is effective in woodland, desert, and urban environments. Soldiers' names are displayed on the ACU and are made of US Army Tape and attached by hook fastener. The Battle Dress Uniform (BDU) contains many of the same items as the ACU, including the same rigger belt, moisture-wicking t-shirt, green socks, and Army combat boots (hot and temperate).

The Improved Physical Fitness Uniform (IPFU) includes six parts: gray or black running jacket, black running pants, black moisture-wicking running trunks, short sleeve moisture-wicking gray t-shirt, long sleeve moisture-wicking gray t-shirt, and knit black cap or micro-fleece green cap. Commanders may authorize the use of commercial workout gear appropriate for the conditions and circumstances, including running shoes, plain white socks without logos, gloves, reflective gear, and long underwear.

Awards and Decorations

The Army recognizes acts of qualifications, special skills, achievements, exceptional service, heroism, and valor through awards and decorations. Awards are decorations, medals, badges, ribbons, and appurtenances bestowed to an individual or unit. Decorations are more individual, recognizing a specific individual act for gallantry or valor. In addition to decorations, individual awards include Good Conduct Medals, Service Medals, Service Ribbons, badges, tabs, certificates, and letters. AR 600-8-22 outlines the DA Military Awards Program, including the procedures and requirements for awards and decorations.

The **Army Service Ribbon** is awarded for completing Basic and AIT. Soldiers may wear a single "V" device at one time, and it may be worn only with the following decorations: Distinguished Flying, Cross Bronze Star Medal, Air Medal, ARCOM, and Joint Service Commendation Medal. Combat experience is recognized with the Combat Infantryman Badge (CIB), Combat Action Badge (CAB), and Combat Medical Badge (CMB).

The **Good Conduct Medal** is awarded to recognize exemplary behavior, efficiency, and fidelity. The company commander must approve the award, and soldiers can receive the Good Conduct Medal only once every 3 years.

The **Medal of Honor** is the highest award that can be achieved during wartime. The award was created during the Civil War, and Private Jacob Parrott became the first recipient on March 25, 1863. The United States Congress must approve a Medal of Honor, and the president of the United States bestows the award. The Medal of Honor has "Valor" inscribed on the suspension bar, and engraved on the reverse side are the recipient's grade, name, and organization. The Roman goddess Minerva is also featured on the Medal of Honor.

The **Purple Heart** is awarded to anyone killed in action against an armed enemy. Unlike other decorations, the Purple Heart doesn't require a recommendation; instead, eligible recipients are entitled to it. Civilians are also eligible to receive the award if they meet the specific criteria. The Purple Heart was originally awarded for valor during the Revolutionary War, making it the first medal awarded in Army history, and the current version features a portrait of George Washington.

Sample Questions and Answers

1. How many campaign streamers were added during the Revolutionary War?

The Army added sixteen campaign streamers during the Revolutionary War.

2. Who needs to provide authorization for a soldier to wear a uniform at a march?

Soldiers need to receive authority from a competent authority before wearing their uniform at a march.

3. What is a command of execution?

A command of execution means the soldier must take the action prescribed by the preceding preparatory command. There is one step or one count in between the preparatory command and command of execution, and a command cannot be altered once the command of execution has been issued.

4. What is AR 600-25?

AR 600-25 governs saluting procedures.

5. Where is the beret positioned in relation to the soldier's eyebrows?

The beret is positioned 1 inch above the soldier's eyebrows with the headband running straight across the forehead.

6. The Medal of Honor was first bestowed during which conflict?

The Medal of Honor was created during the Civil War, and Private Jacob Parrott became the first recipient on March 25, 1863.

7. Where does a soldier halt when saluting a senior officer outside?

The soldier halts 3 steps away from the senior officer before saluting.

8. How many years of service does a stripe represent on both the Army Green Service Uniform and Army Blue Service Uniform?

A stripe represents 3 years of service on both the Army Green Service Uniform and Army Blue Service Uniform.

9. What type of formations do platoons form during ceremonies?

Platoons are arranged in either the line or column formation during ceremonies.

10. The ACU provides effective camouflage in which types of terrain?

The Army Combat Uniform (ACU) provides effective camouflage in the woodland, desert, and urban environments due to its digitized pattern.

11. Does a subordinate need to salute a senior officer when standing in the ranks of a formation?

No, saluting is not required when standing in ranks of a formation.

12. How does a soldier's uniform change after entering the NCO Corps?

After entering the NCO Corps, NCOs wear a service cap instead of a beret headgear and add a gold stripe to the BDU.

13. What is played at the end of retreat?

The National Anthem or "To The Color" is played at the end of retreat as the flag is lowered.

14. Where is the flagpole located at every military installation?

The flagpole is in front of Building Number 1 at every military installation.

15. What is the only decoration that doesn't require a recommendation from a senior officer?

Unlike other decorations, the Purple Heart doesn't require a recommendation because anyone eligible to receive the decoration is entitled to it.

16. Which items are the same in the ACU and BDU?

The BDU and ACU both include the same rigger belt, moisture-wicking t-shirt, green socks, and Army combat boots (hot and temperate).

17. What is AR 600-8-22?

AR 600-8-22 governs the DA Military Awards Program.

18. What form did the hand salute take in Colonial America?

During the Colonial Era in America, the salute involved removing a hat, and it has since evolved into the hand salute.

19. The Purple Heart was first awarded during what conflict?

The Purple Heart was originally awarded for valor during the Revolutionary War, making it the first medal awarded in Army history.

20. What is the one exceptional circumstance where the American flag can be dipped as a salute?

The flag can be dipped as a salute only when friendly ships of war meet at sea.

21. What are the customs surrounding the song "The Army Goes Rolling Along"?

"The Army Goes Rolling Along" is typically played at the end of reviews, parades, and honor guard ceremonies, and every soldier must stand and sing all the lyrics.

22. What is the exception for commercial headgear?

Soldiers cannot wear commercial headgear with an Army uniform except when operating motorcycles and other similar vehicles.

23. What do the stars and stripes on the American flag represent?

The stars represent the fifty states, and the thirteen stripes represent the original Thirteen Colonies.

24. When reporting to a senior officer, how long does the subordinate hold their salute?

Salutes must be held until the senior officer completely drops their hand after returning the salute.

25. Who may authorize the use of commercial workout gear with the IPFU?

Commanders may authorize the use of commercial workout gear with the IPFU, including running shoes, plain white socks without logos, gloves, reflective gear, and long underwear.

26. How many rest commands are there?

There are four rest commands: parade rest, stand at ease, at ease, and rest.

27. When do soldiers wear headgear indoors?

Headgear is worn indoors only when the soldier is under arms in an official capacity or has been directed to wear headgear by the commander.

28. What does blue represent on the American flag?

Blue is included on the American flag to represent vigilance, perseverance, and justice.

29. What is FM 3-21.5?

FM 3-21.5 governs drill and ceremony.

30. What command is used to reverse the unit's direction?

Rear March is the command used to reverse the unit's direction.

Dear Customer,

We would like to start by thanking you for purchasing this study guide. We hope that we exceeded your expectations.

Our goal in creating this study guide was to cover all of the topics that you will encounter on the test. We also strove to make our practice questions as similar as possible to what you will encounter on test day. With that being said, if you found something that you feel was not up to your standards, please send us an email and let us know.

We have study guides in a wide variety of fields. If you're interested in one, try searching for it on Amazon or send us an email.

Thanks Again and Happy Testing!
Product Development Team
info@studyguideteam.com

Interested in buying more than 10 copies of our product?
Contact us about bulk discounts:

bulkorders@studyguideteam.com

FREE Test Taking Tips DVD Offer

To help us better serve you, we have developed a Test Taking Tips DVD that we would like to give you for FREE. **This DVD covers world-class test taking tips that you can use to be even more successful when you are taking your test.**

All that we ask is that you email us your feedback about your study guide. Please let us know what you thought about it – whether that is good, bad or indifferent.

To get your **FREE Test Taking Tips DVD**, email freedvd@studyguideteam.com with "FREE DVD" in the subject line and the following information in the body of the email:

> a. The title of your study guide.

> b. Your product rating on a scale of 1-5, with 5 being the highest rating.

> c. Your feedback about the study guide. What did you think of it?

> d. Your full name and shipping address to send your free DVD.

If you have any questions or concerns, please don't hesitate to contact us at freedvd@studyguideteam.com.

Thanks again!

Made in the USA
Middletown, DE
27 January 2020